Ten Motivating Tips

Here are ten quick and easy tips for getting yourself motivated right now:

- **Begin with the end in mind.** Knowing where you're heading allows you to steer a clear path and achieve your goal.

- **Know where to start.** Choosing a simple step first gives you encouragement and a positive feeling to keep you moving forward to the next step.

- **Keep on track.** Checking your progress helps you to see how you're getting on and lets you make adjustments if needed, helping you to reach your goal.

- **Believe in yourself.** Having faith in yourself and your inner strength helps you make positive changes that feel right for you.

- **Motivate your team.** This tip helps everyone feel happier, more involved, and more productive. (Chapter 11 gives you some ways to motivate team-mates.)

- **Ask for support from colleagues and friends.** Going to people you know and trust can greatly help you. You already know each other so there are no barriers.

- **Take a positive outlook.** Being positive helps your unconscious mind to focus on seeing a way around the challenge.

- **Reward your achievements.** Saying 'well done' to yourself can make you feel great and gives you the encouragement and incentive to keep going.

- **Have the strength to change tack.** Making a change is a positive action rather than staying stuck in a rut. Changing tack can often help you see different and more effective approaches to keeping you moving forward.

- **Visualise your success and see a positive end goal.** Visualising a situation helps you rehearse an event in your mind before it happens, allowing your body and mind to drive you towards your goal because you've already practised succeeding. (Chapter 6 tells you about visualising success.)

Visualising the Benefits of Motivation

Visualisation is about making use of all your senses: what you're seeing, hearing, feeling, tasting, and smelling. Visualising a situation heightens your motivation and allows your mind and body to experience your success before it actually happens. Here's how to visualise:

- **See your success.** Imagine you're painting an image of what you want to achieve. Ensure you clearly see yourself in the picture, then add colour to brighten the picture and bring in action, as if you're the lead actor in a movie.

- **Feel the benefits.** Imagine your feelings as you achieve your goal. You can feel sensations in your body, positive inner thoughts, and strong emotions. Be aware where the feelings are in your body. Injecting positive feelings helps strengthen the visualisation further.

- **Hear the praise.** Enhance and intensify your image further by hearing words of praise or even the sound of people clapping and cheering you. You feel yourself glowing with success from hearing what people are saying about you.

You can read more about visualisation in Chapter 6

Motivation For Dummies®

Creating a Motivational Environment

Your surroundings can have a strong influence on how you feel. Distractions can affect your motivation and stop you getting on with what you need to do. Think about:

- **Lighting:** Natural daylight, sunshine, or full spectrum light are all ideal for keeping you stimulated.

- **Sound:** Some people like working with background noise or having music playing. Others are distracted by the hum of office equipment, people talking, or noise of traffic from outside. Decide which sounds you find bearable and cut out the rest.

- **Space and view:** You may need to rearrange furniture to give yourself more space. Having an untidy and cluttered desk can be very distracting and slows you up. Having windows you can open and shut, and a nice view, all help to create positive feelings about your surroundings.

- **Colour:** Try adding colour and pictures to your walls to help brighten you up and keep you feeling cheerful and stimulated.

- **Seating:** Make sure your chair is comfortable and at the right height for you, especially for when you're working at your computer. The position you sit in can make a difference to your breathing, your posture, and how awake and alert you feel while working.

- **Equipment:** Make sure you have all the equipment you need for your task, so that you're not being distracted by having to stop to find the right tools.

- **Fresh air:** If your office is in the basement, or the windows in your office aren't the sort you can open and shut, make sure you have air-conditioning installed.

- **Temperature:** Make sure you can control the temperature of the room where you're working. Find out where the thermostat is and how to adjust the room temperature if needed.

Chapter 3 goes into more depth about creating a motivational environment.

Plan to Take Action

Taking positive action helps you overcome barriers and keeps you moving forward. Here are some general tips to help your planning.

- **Decide what your first steps are going to be, even writing a 'to do' list first!** Your first steps are the mini-goals to achieving your end goal.

- **Know what's going to keep you motivated: a deadline, family pressure, fear of failure.** Having a timescale is wonderful for keeping you focused.

- **Make sure you have the time available for your task.** Commit time in your diary, prioritise, and stop putting off what you want to achieve.

- **Get into a positive frame of mind.** Feeling positive gives you the momentum to take action and believe that the task is worthwhile.

- **Tell yourself you need to have a positive outcome.** For some people having a positive outcome is more important than for others. Decide if a specific outcome could make all the difference for you.

- **Make sure you can afford what you are setting out to achieve.** Don't let the cost be a barrier to achieving your goal. If money is a problem, try to find cheaper alternatives or ways of overcoming your financial problems.

- **You need to have the right skills for your task.** You may need to think about acquiring new skills, updating your current skills, or asking other people for help.

Chapter 4 tells you more about planning and summoning motivation.

For Dummies: Bestselling Book Series for Beginners

Motivation FOR DUMMIES®

by Gillian Burn

John Wiley & Sons, Ltd

Motivation For Dummies®

Published by **John Wiley & Sons, Ltd**
The Atrium
Southern Gate
Chichester
West Sussex
PO19 8SQ
England

E-mail (for orders and customer service enq

Visit our Home Page on www.wiley.com

For general information on our other products and services, please contact our Customer Care Department within the U.S. at 800-762-2974, outside the U.S. at 317-572-3993, or fax 317-572-4002.

For technical support, please visit www.wiley.com/techsupport.

Wiley also publishes its books in a variety of electronic formats. Some content that appears in print may not be available in electronic books.

British Library Cataloguing in Publication Data: A catalogue record for this book is available from the British Library

ISBN: 978-0-470-76035-2

Printed and bound in Great Britain by TJ International, Padstow, Cornwall

10 9 8 7 6 5 4 3 2 1

WILEY

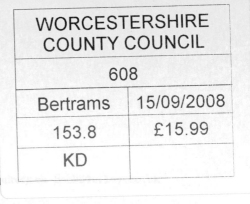

About the Author

Gillian Burn is a health consultant, coach, and trainer. She specialises in enabling individuals and companies to improve their energy and personal effectiveness by focusing on enhancing health and quality of life. She is the editor of *Personal Development All-in-One For Dummies* and the author of two management pocketbooks – the *Energy and Well-Being Pocketbook* and the *NLP Pocketbook*.

Gillian's health career started in nursing, midwifery, and health visiting, alongside a period working with the Flying Doctor Service in the Australian outback. Her business career began with BUPA, a major health care company, designing programmes to improve health at work and reduce sickness absence. Gillian's management experience covered sales, marketing, team management, and product design for health-at-work initiatives delivered to major organisations throughout the UK.

Gillian is director of her own company – Health Circles Ltd – providing a range of well-being and motivation initiatives for companies throughout the UK and Europe. Her training programmes include exercise, nutrition, stress and time management, communication, and creating peak energy. She also runs personal effectiveness courses, including mind mapping® and speed reading.

Passionate about supporting people to boost their energy, creativeness, and motivation, Gillian believes that everyone has the skills and talent to make positive changes to enable them to reach their full potential and peak performance.

Author's Acknowledgements

Writing this book has given me the opportunity to put into practice all the tips, tools, and ideas I have believed in to keep me on track and maintain my own motivation.

To my family, clients, colleagues, Pilates students, and fellow trainers, thank you for your stories, anecdotes, inspiration, and support.

To the whole team at Wiley, including Sam, Wejdan, and Steve, who have kept me on track and provided gentle guidance and encouragement throughout the project.

To my partner John for his amazing encouragement to help me on the whole journey and for your patience for the hours I have been attached to the computer.

Finally, and most importantly, I want to thank my colleague Liz Harris, whose editorial advice and continual support has been tremendous and a wonderful guiding voice throughout the whole project.

Publisher's Acknowledgements

We're proud of this book; please send us your comments through our Dummies online registration form located at www.dummies.com/register/.

Some of the people who helped bring this book to market include the following:

Acquisitions, Editorial, and Media Development

Project Editor: Steve Edwards

Content Editor: Nicole Burnett

Executive Editor: Samantha Spickernell

Development Editor: Kelly Ewing

Commissioning Editor: Samantha Spickernell

Copy Editor: Christine Lea

Proofreader: Helen Heyes

Technical Editor: Averil Leimon

Publisher: Jason Dunne

Executive Project Editor: Daniel Mersey

Cover Photos: © Ron Chapple Stock/Alamy

Cartoons: Ed McLachlan

Composition Services

Project Coordinator: Lynsey Stanford

Layout and Graphics: Reuben W. Davis, Nikki Gately, Melissa K. Jester, Christine Williams

Proofreaders: John Greenough

Indexer: Christine Spina Krapeles

Brand Reviewer: Carrie Burchfield

Contents at a Glance

Table of Contents

Introduction

*M*otivation is all about having the willpower to get started – and once you get going it can direct your life in many ways. It's possible to feel more motivated at some stages of your life than at others, or that your motivation is being affected by other people and events around you. You may even be asking yourself how well motivated you are and whether you could be better!

Motivation For Dummies helps you understand the key elements of motivation and how motivation influences your behaviour and achieving your goals. I've designed each chapter to help you apply the principles of motivation to different areas of your life in a variety of situations, with stories, activities, and exercises to help you along the way. I encourage you to jump in, use the tools, and have a go. Often you find what you're looking for while trying out new ideas.

So, hop on board and get started on your journey to a more motivated life.

About This Book

When you look up 'motivation' in a dictionary you find a list of alternative meanings, such as encourage, stimulate, spur, energise. If you search on the Internet, you can expect to find over 55 million references to motivation linked to sport, work, business, personal life, and that's just a start! There are also over a million references to books about motivation, bringing home to you the depth and breadth of the subject, and the variety of ways you can use motivation in your life.

Your task ahead is to pinpoint which areas of your life are going to benefit from you being more motivated. This means looking closely at your situation to see where you can or need to make changes. Motivation can help you to:

- Boost your energy to achieve your goals
- Summon up your enthusiasm to get started
- Understand what's getting in your way
- Change direction or behave differently

- ✔ Make your job more inspirational
- ✔ Show you how and when to get into action
- ✔ Realign your relationships in your work and personal life
- ✔ Positively influence your health and wellbeing

Conventions Used in This Book

To highlight particular points and make your reading easier, I've set up a few conventions:

- ✔ *Italics* are used for emphasis and to introduce new terms.
- ✔ **Bold** text is used to indicate the key idea in a list.
- ✔ `Monofont` text is used for website and email addresses to make them stand out.

What You're Not to Read

This book is intended as a hands-on guide to motivation. If you're pushed for time, you don't need to read *everything* in the book from cover to cover. In particular, you can skip:

- ✔ **The text in the sidebars:** the shaded boxes that appear here and there contain extra information or stories and anecdotes – nice to read but not essential to the topic in hand, so you can safely skip them if you're not interested.
- ✔ **The stuff on the copyright page:** you'll find nothing here of interest unless you're looking for legal notices and reprint information. If you are, then this is the place to look!

Foolish Assumptions

When writing this book, I made a few assumptions about you. I'm assuming that you're a normal human being who wants to be happy and motivated. You're keen to find out how you can improve various areas of your life and how getting motivated can help you achieve your goals.

How This Book Is Organised

The book is divided into five parts so you can quickly see what you need to know at any moment. The Table of Contents gives you the full details of what's in each chapter.

Part I: Understanding the Basics of Motivation

In this part, I explain what I mean by motivation and how it can impact on your everyday life. You explore the psychology of motivation and how you can apply the theories to real-life situations. You also discover how to prepare yourself for motivation by highlighting your priorities, tuning into your brain, and creating a motivating environment for yourself.

Part II: Identifying and Maintaining Change

Knowing how to summon up the motivation to change and plan for action is a key starting point. You also explore how to face your demons and deal with setbacks so that you can set goals and keep yourself motivated in the long term.

Part III: Arming Yourself with Motivational Tools

In this part, I show you the tools you need to help get you motivated. You take a journey inside your brain and look at ways of stimulating your motivation using some of the techniques of Neuro-linguistic Programming. You also take a look at incentives and rewards to find out how they work in keeping you motivated.

Part IV: Using Motivation in Different Areas of Your Life

In this part, you look at how you can use motivation in your personal relationships, the workplace, and in your career. You also take a look at how motivation affects your health and wellbeing, and how motivation can help you develop and grow when changing direction or responding to new challenges.

Part V: The Part of Tens

This is where you go for a few ideas for keeping yourself or your team at work motivated. I suggest some fun exercises, tips, and ideas to keep you moving forward, and some actions you can take every day to keep yourself motivated. You can also read the stories of ten inspirational and highly motivated people who can act as your role models.

Appendix

The Appendix contains a selection of additional resources, including books and training websites, that you can also use to help you on your motivation journey.

Icons Used in This Book

Some information in this book is so important and interesting that it's highlighted by an icon.

Here you find human interest stories that you may find inspiring or useful.

The bull's-eye highlights practical advice you can use as an on-the-spot motivation booster.

This icon gives you an exercise to do to give you the chance of experiencing what it feels like to be motivated.

Take special note of the information I give you here and keep it in mind as you apply the principles of motivation in your life.

Where to Go from Here

Turning to the next page takes you straight into an explanation of motivation. But you don't have to start at Chapter 1 and keep going to the end. You may decide that certain topics are more interesting or are more meaningful for you at the moment. So, look them up in the Index and flip to the relevant page. You can also use the Table of Contents at the front of the book to see what catches your fancy.

If, after reading *Motivation For Dummies*, you're keen for more, take a look at the further guidance and resources I recommend at www.healthcircles.co.uk.

Part I
Understanding the Basics of Motivation

'You said you needed something bigger to
motivate you, Bagwort, so we're transferring
you to the elephant house.'

In this part. . .

*H*ere you set off on your motivation journey. You begin to understand what motivation is all about, look at the principles of motivation, and find out how motivation fits into your life. You also explore the psychology behind motivation. So, don't hold back a minute longer, get moving!

Chapter 1

Introducing Motivation

. . . .

. . . .

Getting yourself motivated to achieve a desired goal lies at the heart of your success. In this chapter, you discover what being motivated means, how motivation can help you, and the way your brain and body interact to keep you fully motivated.

Figuring Out What Motivation Is

Motivation is a feeling, an emotional force, stimulating and encouraging you to do something. You feel motivated by factors or stimuli – internal or external – rousing you into action and fulfilling a need:

> ✔ **Internal:** Feeling hungry motivates you to eat – an intrinsic need coming from inside yourself.
>
> ✔ **External:** Showing poor sales results motivates you to attract more clients to increase business – an extrinsic need coming from outside yourself.

Think of a time when you felt highly motivated in your job. You enjoyed going to work and having a sense of achievement at seeing your projects come to fruition. Your efforts were rewarded with a good salary; you had support from your manager, and the authority to make your own decisions. You got along well with your colleagues and delighted in the office camaraderie. You felt valued and that you contributed to the success of the business.

The key motivators at work in this instance are: achieving success, financial reward, camaraderie, and feeling valued.

Here are three real-life examples of internal and external stimuli:

✔ Daniel runs a small hotel business, which has been in his family for three generations. It's hard work, involves long hours, and isn't hugely financially rewarding. The stimuli that help Daniel maintain his motivation to keep the business going are both intrinsic and extrinsic. Intrinsically he feels it's important to uphold the family tradition as hoteliers. It satisfies his sense of continuity and staying faithful to his roots. The extrinsic stimulus comes from his staff. Daniel feels responsible for his staff and their livelihoods, particularly as several of them have been with his business for many years.

✔ A teacher friend of mine tutors children to help them improve their reading skills. She told me how positive and motivated she felt when, just after one session, the other teachers commented on how they'd noticed an improvement in the children's reading ability. My friend travels a long way to the school for the sessions, but feels it is worth all the effort to see the improvement in the children's reading skills and hear the positive comments from the teachers. Her initial success stimulated her motivation to keep up the good work as well as giving her the feeling that she's really making a difference.

✔ I have been a member of a rowing club on the Thames for several years. Soon after joining the club I took part in a competition called a scratch regatta. On the day of the regatta the names of each crew were picked out of a hat, mixing together novice and experienced rowers. I rowed with three other people of varying abilities. On winning the first race we felt great. Then we went on to win the second and third rounds and make it into the final. When we went over the finishing line first I was elated. I can still remember how excited I felt receiving the trophy, and how motivated I felt to keep up my rowing. What motivated me was a combination of three factors: enjoying the team work, winning the competition, and receiving the trophy. That motivation has stayed with me ever since!

You can also be motivated because of the consequences of *not* doing something. For example, the fear of a financial penalty through missing the deadline for your tax return motivates you to complete it on time. Or, the humiliation at not being able to wear your favourite outfits because you have put on a lot of weight motivates you to join a slimming club.

Motivation is the force driving you forward to make a change, for example, toward a goal (looking fit and healthy), or away from something you want to change (being overweight and unfit).

ANECDOTE

Different motivators for different people

On 31 January 2008, approximately 300,000 people in the UK were busy trying to file their self-assessment tax returns online, having known about this deadline since 5 April 2007, but choosing to leave filling in their tax returns until the last possible moment. Many people worked throughout the night to beat the deadline and avoid a financial penalty. The sheer volume of users of the system that night caused the system to fail, and 100,000 returns couldn't be submitted! The Government had to extend the deadline by 24 hours in order to get the computer system up and running again. The moral of this story: plan well in advance!

In this instance the fear of the financial penalty was a poor motivator, as many people missed the deadline. A more positive motivator could have been the offer of a rebate of £200 for anyone completing the return early. HM Revenue & Customs now actually use this approach, offering individuals a £150 incentive for completing their self-assessment tax forms online rather than by using traditional paper copies.

In January 2008, a relatively unknown English non-league football club, Havant and Waterlooville, won their FA Cup competition game unexpectedly. This gave them the chance of a lifetime to play against Liverpool, a premier league football team, in the Liverpool stadium. Liverpool had won the European Cup more times than any other English side and had several world-class players in their team. In contrast, the Havant and Waterlooville team was made up of part-time players having day jobs such as electricians and plumbers.

The day Havant and Waterlooville went to Liverpool was no different for them than for Liverpool. Havant and Waterlooville were defeated, but had a very respectable 5:2 score and received a standing ovation at the end of the game from the Liverpool players and the 42,000 spectators. Havant and Waterlooville had played better than anyone could've imagined.

The support Havant and Waterlooville received that day from their own 6,000 fans at Liverpool, and their sense of achievement from playing there, will, I am sure, stay with each player for the rest of their lives and motivate them in their future careers. Havant and Waterlooville's team success has to be a powerful motivating factor for budding football players striving to achieve their dreams.

Knowing How to Maintain Motivation

Understanding what factors keep you motivated is important to achieving your goal. The factors can differ from one person to another. Specific factors motivating you may include the following:

- ✔ Your desire for order motivates you to clear your desk and file away your old papers.
- ✔ Keeping up with your mates on the football pitch at the weekend motivates you to keep fit.

✔ The personal satisfaction a sports coach gets from seeing a dramatic improvement in a player's game motivates the coach to keep up the good work.

✔ A manager is motivated to encourage and applaud his team more often after seeing the glow on the face of a team member receiving praise from a client.

On a recent holiday to Europe, I had a relaxing time people-watching. People were strolling around apparently motivated to be out of doors by the warm sunshine and brilliant blue sky. I noticed women shopping and drinking coffee together in a calm, relaxed manner, obviously enjoying each other's company. People sat in the parks reading and breathing in the fresh air. Children played happily, busy exploring their surroundings. The shops closed in the afternoon, allowing people to take a long lunch followed by a siesta before returning to work in the early evening. Everyone seemed relaxed, happy, and motivated while going about their daily business.

Being caught up in the rush hour in London on a cold and wet winter's day made a startling contrast. I noticed everyone was rushing and pushing to get to the head of the line. Strain and pressure were etched on long faces. People appeared to be motivated to get home as quickly as possible, rather than slowing down and enjoying their surroundings.

Recognising How Motivation Helps You

Feeling motivated can improve your health and have a positive effect on your family and relationships. The more motivated you feel, the greater your energy and enthusiasm for getting on with your everyday activities.

Being motivated helps you to take on tasks, reach targets, meet deadlines, complete projects, and achieve your goals. Reaching a goal can motivate you to achieve even more, creating a positive cumulative effect.

Here are some benefits of motivation:

✔ **Being part of a group:** You can feel motivated simply by being part of a group or team. The group can be a family unit, work colleagues, a sports team, or the group of friends you socialise with. Being in a group provides support, allowing you to talk about problems, give and receive encouragement and friendship.

✔ **Being on your own:** You may be motivated to work alone on a task to satisfy your creativity or need time to reflect without distractions from others.

✔ **Being inspired by role models:** Having a role model can be inspiring and motivating. For example, a sports star can motivate you to improve your performance. (For more on the importance of role models, see the sidebar 'How role models can make a difference'.)

✔ **Being in control:** Motivation gives you the sense of being in control. When you're motivated, you quickly understand what the task involves, how to set about it, and when to start. Solving problems is easier the more motivated you are. Rather than a problem being a barrier, you have the confidence and motivation to see past the problem and discover alternatives.

The more motivated you are, the more prepared you are to face a challenge, rather than giving up at the first hurdle.

✔ **Passing motivation onto others:** When you're motivated, you pass on your positive feeling to those around you, making other people feel inspired and motivated. Conversely, if you feel unmotivated, people around you may detect your lack of motivation and apathy, affecting the way they respond to you.

While writing this book, I discussed the subject of motivation with as many different people as possible to get an insight into their experiences. After talking about motivation to one particular friend, I discovered that she now feels more motivated to work through tasks that have been piling up for several months – if not years! She analysed what motivated her at a subconscious level and the personal barriers that were keeping her unmotivated. After getting to grips with her outstanding jobs, she felt good in herself, and motivated to achieve even more.

How role models can make a difference

A TV series called *Make Your Child Brilliant* showed how people can have a strong motivating effect on young children, especially when a hidden talent is identified and harnessed. The education guru Bernadette Tynan was on the show, focusing on finding the hidden talents in children.

In one particular show an 11-year-old girl called Molly was given 'brain-training' techniques to help her carry out the challenge of making a presentation to a large group of people. Molly worked closely with Bernadette Tynan and her parents on a variety of techniques to give her the confidence and the skills she needed. Molly had to do her own research, choose her props, and deliver a story about the complexities of marine life and evolution.

On the day of the presentation, Molly stood before her audience of over 120 people, speaking confidently into the microphone without notes and using her props effectively. Her presentation was superb and she outshone many people twice her age. She had been motivated by the support of Bernadette and her parents to tackle this daunting challenge, while acquiring a variety of 'brain-training' techniques that she would be able to use throughout her life.

Coming alive when talking about your favourite subject

A friend's son is studying physics at university. He's not the most communicative person I know and sometimes it's quite difficult to know what he's thinking or to get him to say much at all. That is until he gets talking about physics! He then comes alive and talks non-stop – motivated by the complexities of the subject that leaves many of us behind. His usual lack of confidence disappears when he's speaking on a subject he's passionate about.

Identifying the Barriers

Barriers can slow down your motivation or even put a stop on your actions completely. Recognising the barriers is the first step to overcoming them.

For example, one of my friends kept on putting off tackling her backlog of tasks because she was only motivated to get down to them on days when she had no fixed appointments or commitments. But finding a clear day was creating a barrier. She had tried squeezing the various tasks on her to-do list into the odd hour between meetings and appointments but without success. Then she hit on the idea of rearranging her diary to fit her meetings into the one day, thereby freeing up the other days for other important tasks. Having the luxury of a clear day without the pressure of meetings motivated her into dealing swiftly with her backlog.

Once my friend faced up to her barrier she was able to move forward. She was now motivated to:

- ✔ Book time with a DIY expert to fix the jobs around her home that had been piling up
- ✔ Find the courage to pick up the phone to contact people she'd previously been making excuses not to call
- ✔ Plan time in her diary for regular exercise and stick firmly to it

A variety of barriers can affect your motivation:

- ✔ **Distractions:** Being inundated with emails, meetings, and interruptions from people can affect how motivated you feel, both positively and negatively.

✔ **Family commitments:** Having family commitments, such as caring for an elderly relative, can be difficult and demotivating, stopping you putting time aside for yourself and your tasks.

✔ **Finances:** Shortage of money can affect your motivation to do something if you feel you can't afford it. However, a financial reward for completing a task is a big motivating factor. And the opportunity of earning more money can motivate you into changing your career path.

✔ **Home environment:** Your home environment can have a demotivating effect (see Chapter 4). Living in an untidy, cluttered, disorganised working space can act as a barrier to getting yourself motivated for action.

✔ **Illness or poor health:** When you're ill, your energy is reduced and it's harder to feel motivated to do the jobs you need to do. Being patient and giving yourself time to get over your illness may be necessary to restore you to full health and feeling fully motivated again.

✔ **Keeping to rigid rules or procedures:** Some employees may lack motivation if red tape, rules, and procedures stop them being creative. Conversely, some employees need rules and procedures to create boundaries in which they feel comfortable working.

Employers beware! Find out what motivates your staff and whether too many boundaries or too few could be stifling motivation and creativity.

✔ **Lack of support:** Lack of support from colleagues or friends can act as a barrier, taking away your enthusiasm to tackle certain tasks.

✔ **Timing:** You can feel more motivated at certain times of the year, for example at New Year, in the spring, or when you're going on holiday. Some people are motivated to work harder in the mornings rather than later in the day. Their body clock is programmed to give them more energy at certain times.

✔ **Weather conditions:** You can easily feel a lack of motivation to go out for a walk when the weather is cold, wet, and windy. In contrast, on a hot, sunny day you may find it harder to feel motivated to work when you would prefer to be outdoors.

For example, a manager on a recent course I ran described how he regularly received 250 to 300 emails a day. This distracted him from his day-to-day responsibilities and he decided to put in place a clear procedure to stop himself feeling overwhelmed and to maintain his motivation for his job. He prioritised his emails, flagging up the urgent ones and taking action and deleting others at certain times of the day, giving himself the time to focus on the demands of his job and worldwide responsibilities. By sticking to his plan, the sheer volume of emails was managed, allowing him to work productively.

ANECDOTE

Giving up smoking. . . or not

Jayne was getting on really well with her no-smoking campaign. She had felt motivated to give up smoking after a friend fell seriously ill. From that point Jayne vowed to become a non-smoker. She'd managed without a cigarette for nearly three months.

Then Jayne unexpectedly lost her job. She felt very unhappy and wasn't sure where to look for a new job. The security her job gave her, and the support from her colleagues, kept her motivated in her no-smoking campaign. After losing her job, she lost direction. Feeling low,

she comforted herself with a cigarette. Within a couple of days, she was back to smoking regularly again. She had lost the motivation to continue her no-smoking campaign.

When Jayne smoked, it gave her a feeling of security and the ability to deal with anxiety. When she gave up smoking, she replaced this positive by-product with the support from her colleagues and the security from her job. On losing her job, Jayne quite naturally went back to smoking.

Looking Into Your Brain or Body for Answers

Your mind holds the answers to many of life's mysteries and secrets. The psychology of motivation looks into your inner feelings and internal state, driving you forward to feel motivated, or stopping you in your tracks.

What's going on in your mind is often expressed through the actions of your body. If you feel motivated or demotivated inside, your body reacts accordingly on the outside. For example, you display signs of happiness and pleasure when doing something enjoyable, or blind panic when you know you have to do something you dread.

Try visualising that feeling of motivation within your body as if it is a freely flowing stream, an athlete performing at the height of his abilities, or driving a car on a road without any traffic.

What motivation feels like

You can experience the feeling of motivation in a variety of ways. Some people describe motivation as feeling good, being propelled into action, and happy to tackle more. Other people actually sense or feel motivation within their body, almost as if they can touch the very spot that feels motivated. A friend usually feels motivation around the centre of her body. Other people experience motivation from how they behave. Your feeling of motivation can be similar to a well-balanced car: well tuned and firing on all cylinders.

Equally, a feeling of being unbalanced, disharmony, or fear can motivate you into action.

If you have difficulty experiencing what it feels like to be motivated, picture a party balloon soaring into the sky with the wind taking it higher and higher. Motivation can give you that same kind of feeling inside your body and a sense of elation.

Some people enjoy the feeling of motivation from actually doing the task, others from achieving the end result. For example, your love of gardening motivates you to go outside and get digging. Or, your motivation may come from imagining beautifully mown lawns and neat borders after the work is done.

An acquaintance told me that feeling motivated was like adrenaline pumping through his body, a bubbling sense of excitement as he progressed toward his goal. Another person described how she once experienced motivation as the sensation of tiny involuntary shaking movements throughout her body, a bit like pins and needles.

On the other side of the coin, feelings of demotivation can be explored by tuning into your body to find answers to make you feel motivated again.

The motivating effect of an extreme challenge

A TV programme called *Extreme Survival* took a number of ordinary people away from their normal lives on a trip through the Ugandan rainforest and jungle, before tackling a tough climb up Mount Baker. The climb, involving ascending over 15,000 feet, was an astonishing challenge for the participants because none of them had ever climbed before, let alone experienced climbing in very demanding conditions and coping with the effects of altitude. The elation one of the climbers felt when she reached the top of Mount Baker was written all over her face, showing how proud she was, having proved to herself that she could reach such dizzy heights. Another participant who was, in his own words, a very unhealthy, overweight, and unfit taxi driver, on reaching the summit said he felt such an adrenaline buzz and sense of elation that he was motivated to leave his old unhealthy life behind.

The expedition proved to be highly motivating for all the participants. Having conquered the summit of the mountain, they had an immense sense of achievement, giving them a new lease of life, and motivating them to approach their lives from then on in a positive way.

Watching for signs of demotivation

Facial expressions can signal what and how a person is feeling. You may notice a lack of energy or enthusiasm, or the person who's usually lively and communicative is suddenly withdrawn and quiet. The colour of a person's skin can also act as a clue. If someone is feeling demotivated, the skin can look pale, as if all the colour is draining out of his face.

Feelings of demotivation can also be expressed by how your body is reacting. Energy levels appear low, the person seems lethargic and lacks get up and go.

Signs and symptoms of demotivation and feeling off-balance can include the following:

- ✔ Not sleeping well
- ✔ Feeling overwhelmed
- ✔ Illness
- ✔ Irritability
- ✔ Being uncommunicative
- ✔ Feeling under pressure
- ✔ Finding barriers or obstacles to situations

ANECDOTE

Turning demotivation into a plan

A colleague was concerned about Anna, a member of his team. He noticed that Anna wasn't as jovial and happy around the office as usual. Her facial expression showed a lack of enthusiasm when he discussed forthcoming projects with her. After watching Anna's behaviour for a couple of weeks, my colleague took the time to talk to her privately to find out what was behind her lack of motivation.

As he listened to Anna describing the last few weeks, he discovered that a new member of the team lay at the heart of Anna's problem. The new team member had been spending a lot of time with Anna being trained, needing her to explain procedures and constantly interrupting Anna throughout her working day. Anna was struggling to get her own work done, but also wanted to help her new team member.

As Anna talked through her situation, she solved the problem herself by deciding to set aside certain times of each day to train the new employee. This gave Anna the time to work on her own projects without interruption. After the conversation with my colleague, Anna felt much more positive. She worked out a solution herself but, most importantly, had regained her sense of motivation and enjoyment in her job. This fact was evident from her facial expressions because she went back to looking her cheerful and happy self.

Your inner voice frequently tells you what you need to change to get back on track and feel motivated again.

Tune into your body to discover what motivates you. When you feel motivated, look at how your body is reacting. Enjoy the sensation and allow that feeling to move you forward to your next project or task.

Chapter 2

Exploring the Psychology of Motivation

In This Chapter

▶ Identifying the stages of motivation

▶ Coming to grips with the psychology

▶ Testing the theories

Knowing something about the theories behind motivation can help you get to the bottom of why, from time to time, you find yourself struggling to keep motivated. In this chapter, I explore different theories of motivation and how you can apply them to your particular situation.

Understanding the Stages of Motivation

Researchers in the mid-1950s came up with the theory that factors such as physical wellbeing, relationships, and status influenced, directed, energised, and underpinned human behaviour.

Exploring Maslow's theory

Abraham Maslow is one of the founders of the human potential movement. In 1954, he brought together a large body of research about motivation, showing how some people are prepared to go through fire and water to achieve, even though the odds are stacked against them – while other people stay just as they are!

Maslow's theories are seen as landmarks in the psychology of motivation. (You can read about the link with Maslow and confidence in *Building Confidence For Dummies* by Kate Burton.)

Maslow introduced the theory of the 'hierarchy of human needs', showing different forces that motivate individuals. The hierarchy has five levels:

- ✔ Physiological
- ✔ Safety
- ✔ Love and belonging
- ✔ Esteem
- ✔ Self-actualisation

Maslow's hierarchy of human needs (see Figure 2-1) shows the importance of each level to motivation. Maslow points out that the lowest level, *physiological*, is the strongest motivator because basic human needs, such as food and water, have to be met before any other desires can surface and before moving up the hierarchy to the next level. On reaching the highest level, *self-actualisation*, you feel that all your needs have been met, and you know what is really important to you.

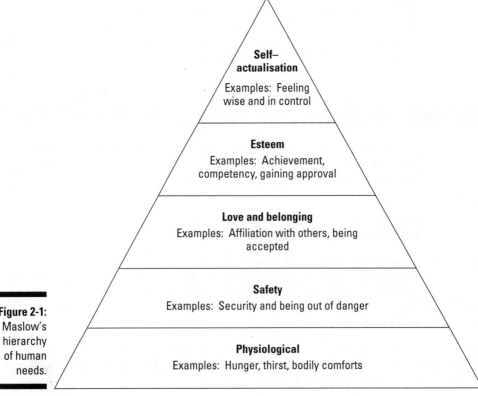

Figure 2-1:
Maslow's
hierarchy
of human
needs.

Relating yourself to each stage

Think about how you relate to each of the five levels and how your motivation is affected.

✔ **Physiological:** You have to meet all your basic needs simply to exist: the air you breathe, water, food, sleep. Having met your physiological needs you can move onto the next stage or level. For example, being lost in the desert and then coming upon a water hole saves your life, allowing you to carry on with your journey. Other examples:

> When lunchtime is approaching, and someone else near you is already eating a sandwich, your motivation dips until you satisfy your fundamental physiological need for food.

> A new baby disturbs your sleep until she falls asleep herself, enabling you to meet your need for rest.

> Transatlantic travel, changing time zones, and sleep deprivation on the plane cause your motivation to dip until you reach your destination and can refresh yourself with food, drink, and sleep. You're only able to move up the hierarchy when these needs are met.

✔ **Safety:** Having satisfied your basic needs you are ready to go onto the next level. Now you need to protect yourself from danger. You're unlikely to be chased by dangerous wild animals nowadays but many everyday experiences can leave you feeling threatened. The fight and flight stress response (see Chapter 7) causes automatic physical responses to come into play. You are only ready to move to the next level when you feel safe and secure. Examples include:

> Walking home with friends after a late party, not really listening to what they are saying until you're safely back in your home.

> During the rush hour you need to get out of the crush before you can think clearly enough to plan the next stage of your journey home.

> Locking all the doors at night before you can relax sufficiently to be able to sleep.

✔ **Love and belonging:** Building up positive relationships with other people and being accepted as part of a group can be vital to your well-being. If these needs aren't met, you can feel isolated and lonely. You thrive when you're being loved and enjoying a sense of belonging. Examples include:

> Joining a new company and only really feeling settled when the existing group invites you to join them for lunch or for evening entertainment.

Being called by your favourite nickname, showing that you're accepted by the group.

Feeling relaxed and at ease with a group of friends so you're able to discuss problems or personal issues.

✔ **Esteem:** Gaining the approval, respect, and recognition of your worth by your family, friends, and colleagues is important for maintaining your self-respect and defines your status in society. Your status carries varying degrees of responsibility in relation to the people around you, for example, as a parent, teacher, doctor, politician, minister, or judge. Examples include:

A colleague asks you to make an impromptu presentation about an area of your work and you feel happy to do it because they acknowledge your expertise.

A local organisation asks you to represent them, due to your status in the community.

A friend asks you for advice, and you feel flattered that she's asked you.

✔ **Self-actualisation:** When you reach this stage all your needs have been met. You're a fully-rounded person, capable of making a positive contribution to society and in control of what you want to do. Your continual striving ends, you can now decide what is truly important in life, and you know what motivates you. For example, you've reached a point where you are ready to share your good fortune with others and give back to society. Examples of this stage include:

A well-paid managing director gives up corporate life to follow his passion to become an artist.

A director relinquishes his role to pursue his interest in charity work.

A doctor leaves the Western world to offer medical aid to an under-developed country.

Maslow's hierarchy of human needs shows that it's possible for you to be operating at different levels or stages at any given time. Your behaviour can vary according to the circumstances. For example, what motivates you on a Sunday morning or Friday afternoon, compared with early on a Monday morning when you are heading to work can vary wildly. Understanding how the five levels affect you is important for knowing what drives you onwards, and for putting you in control of what you want to achieve in your life.

Exploring How the Psychology Can Help

Maslow's theory, described in the preceding section, is a starting point for understanding motivation, and you can apply Maslow's theory to a variety of situations. There are also other psychology theorists who have come up with more ideas that help to address different aspects of motivation.

Hertzberg's hygiene factors

Frederick Hertzberg became famous in 1959 for his 'hygiene' and 'motivational' factors theory. Hertzberg was concerned mainly with the wellbeing of people in the workplace and developed his theory as a management tool, as much as a general theory of motivation.

Hertzberg described hygiene factors as those which only achieve a sense of maintenance or, in other words, that help you maintain basic needs within your job, alongside other factors, which he described as true motivators. These hygiene factors may be the reason you go to work, such as earning a reasonable salary or having good relationships with your colleagues. They don't necessarily encourage you to work harder or more effectively and could also be the cause of dissatisfaction.

Hertzberg's hygiene needs (or maintenance factors) are:

- ✔ Salary
- ✔ Company car
- ✔ Status
- ✔ Security
- ✔ Relationship with supervisor
- ✔ Working conditions
- ✔ Relationship with subordinates

His research shows that people strive to achieve hygiene needs because they are unhappy without them, but once satisfied the effect soon wears off – satisfaction is temporary.

From his research, Hertzberg came to the conclusion that people aren't motivated by addressing hygiene needs alone. The true motivators in the workplace are bound up in job satisfaction, no matter what else the company provides for you. Motivators imposed by the organisation cause employees ultimately to feel dissatisfied. Hertzberg found that workers are motivated by their own internal needs.

A networking experience

Susie joined a networking event for the first time. When she arrived she felt very anxious and unsure and lacked confidence when she was speaking to other members. She then met a couple of people she found it easy to talk to, having common interests and hobbies. She immediately started to feel at ease, regained her confidence, and felt safe in the situation. She attended the meeting each month and soon felt ready to put her name forward to be the next group chairman. She felt she had gained recognition and respect and was ready to take a more active role in the group from the one she experienced on her very first day.

Susie, in her own way, had progressed up Maslow's hierarchy of human needs to get to a level where she felt satisfied with herself and motivated to give back to the group by taking on more responsibility.

Take the example of a company that, for many years, gave all its employees a bottle of champagne and a smoked salmon every Christmas. One year, they decided to stop the gesture because no one had thanked them on the previous years or given any indication that they were grateful or enthusiastic. However, stopping the initiative and not introducing anything in its place caused a great deal of resentment and resulted in a lack of motivation.

Here are Hertzberg's true motivators:

- ✔ Achievement
- ✔ Recognition
- ✔ Work itself
- ✔ Responsibility
- ✔ Advancement
- ✔ Personal growth

Theory X and Theory Y

Theory X and Theory Y were created and developed by Douglas McGregor in the 1960s and have been used in many areas of business management including human resource management, organisational behaviour, and organisational development.

Theory X and Theory Y both state that it is the manager's role to organise resources, including people, for the benefit of the company. However, Theory X and Theory Y each take a very different approach to motivating the workforce. McGregor came to the conclusion that most companies followed one or the other approach.

Theory X

Theory X management assumes that:

- ✔ Employees are naturally lazy and avoid work if they can.

- ✔ Employees show little ambition unless they are given incentives.

- ✔ Workers need to be closely supervised with a system of checks and controls in place.

- ✔ Most workers avoid responsibility and have no ambition; preferring to follow rather than lead.

- ✔ Employees think that it is the manager's job to structure the work and motivate employees.

- ✔ Most employees have no interest in being creative or solving organisational problems.

- ✔ Most employees resist change.

- ✔ Workers are motivated first of all by money, and second by job security.

Theory X managers believe that employees are motivated only by money. If things go wrong in the workplace, a Theory X manager blames the employee first without questioning whether it is the system, company policy, or lack of training that is at fault.

A Theory X manager often stands in the way of employee motivation, productivity, and morale and adopts an authoritarian style of management based on the threat of punishment.

Theory Y

Theory Y management assumes that:

- ✔ People naturally enjoy work.

- ✔ Employees are naturally ambitious and like responsibility.

- ✔ Employees like to be given the opportunity to be creative and forward thinking and not be bogged down by rules.

- ✔ Employees are motivated to meet the organisation's objectives if they are committed to them.

> ✔ Employees are motivated to achieve if rewards are in place that address higher needs, such as self-fulfilment.
>
> ✔ Encouraging creativity results in greater productivity throughout the organisation.

A Theory Y manager believes that giving employees the opportunity of having the satisfaction of doing a good job is a strong motivator in itself. A Theory Y manager tries to remove the barriers that stop workers from reaching self-actualisation.

The reality of Theory X and Theory Y

McGregor's Theory X and Theory Y clearly set out the rules for achieving the organisation's objectives. In reality, most employees (and managers) fall somewhere in between practising the two theories. Theory Y takes a *positive* approach to management and improving the culture of the organisation. Here are a few Theory Y guiding principles to help you in boosting your motivation:

> ✔ Broadening the scope of an employee's job adds variety and opportunity.
>
> ✔ Consulting employees in the decision-making process taps into their creativity and gives employees some control over their work environment.
>
> ✔ Having performance appraisals in place allows employees to take part in checking if they are meeting the organisation's objectives.
>
> ✔ Creating the right circumstances allows employees to achieve a higher level of job satisfaction.

If you are allowed to manage your workload and output you feel more positive and you are more productive. You know better than anyone how to get the best out of yourself. Managers need to be open to a positive view of employees and the possibilities for the organisation that this creates.

Testing the Level of Motivation in Your Work

In *Building Confidence For Dummies*, Kate Burton provides a 'Job Motivation Response Self-Test' to help you measure your motivational responses at work. You can find the self-test in Table 2-1. It takes only a couple of minutes to do and even if you're working on your own, you can change the questions as necessary to suit your own circumstances. Give yourself up to five points for each question – all five if you strongly agree, down to one if you strongly disagree.

Table 2-1	**Job Motivation Response Self-Test**				
Value Statement	**Strongly Agree (5 points)**	**Agree (4 points)**	**Neutral (3 points)**	**Disagree (2 points)**	**Strongly Disagree (1 point)**
I am entirely in control of my work environment. Provided I meet my objectives, I am free to decide how much I do and what work I do next.					
I have established a good working relationship with my boss. She gives me the room to do my job the way I want and I usually deliver what she needs.					
My benefits package and general working environment are okay. When something needs to be looked at, it's usually sorted out in a reasonable time.					

(continued)

Table 2-1 (continued)

Value Statement	Strongly Agree (5 points)	Agree (4 points)	Neutral (3 points)	Disagree (2 points)	Strongly Disagree (1 point)
My work colleagues are generally supportive and don't get in my way. We are a good team and each of us serves the group objective pretty effectively. When issues arise, we are usually able to deal with them.					
I get a real buzz from the work I do. I feel closely identified with my output and put the best of myself into it. I wouldn't want it to be any other way.					
I feel that my employer values my work and is in touch with what is going on. They care about my career and look after things so that I don't have to worry about them.					

Table 2-1 *(continued)*

Value Statement	Strongly Agree (5 points)	Agree (4 points)	Neutral (3 points)	Disagree (2 points)	Strongly Disagree (1 point)
My work is very visible. People know that it is mine, and I take great pride in it. It is not unusual for people to acknowledge the good job I am doing.					
I am allowed to take full responsibility for the quality of my work and for meeting my other objectives and deadlines. My boss knows that I know how to get the best out of myself and lets me get on with it.					
I feel that my work stretches me and allows me to grow. I have the level of challenge and variety that keeps me fully engaged without being overwhelmed.					

(continued)

Table 2-1 *(continued)*

Value Statement	Strongly Agree (5 points)	Agree (4 points)	Neutral (3 points)	Disagree (2 points)	Strongly Disagree (1 point)
My work is an expression of who I truly am at some deeper level. Even if I were not being paid, I would still need to express myself through the kind of work I do. If I were unable to work it would be like losing a limb.					

Taking Your Mind on a Journey

More recent motivational theories focus on *self-efficacy* and what is going on in your mind. Self-efficacy means a person's perception of their ability to reach a goal, as opposed to their self-esteem, which relates to a person's sense of self-worth.

Bandura's self-efficacy theory, dating from 1986 and updated in 1997, puts forward the idea that if a person believes a particular action is possible, then they can achieve it: meaning they believe they are capable of achieving a task or goal.

Unravelling the mystery of Bandura's self-efficacy

Bandura's theory states that 'self-efficacy is the belief in one's capabilities to organise and execute the source of action required to manage prospective situations'. In effect, a person has control over their thoughts, feelings, and actions.

Self-efficacy is the basis of human motivation and personal achievements. If you don't believe you can achieve a desired outcome from your actions, you have little or no incentive to act, or to continue acting when presented with difficulties.

Being able to manage your thoughts and actions makes it easier for you to set, carry out, modify, or even change the direction of your goal.

What people _believe_ influences their motivation and actions. For example, a person may truly believe they have the necessary knowledge and skills to achieve their goal, even though their actual capabilities don't match up to the situation.

Even a very talented person who is capable of performing and exceeding the assigned task can suffer extreme self-doubt if their self-efficacy is low. In contrast, another person can be extremely confident about what they want to accomplish despite having limited skills, while having very high self-efficacy.

Your level of self-efficacy goes a long way in helping you to achieve your goals.

Low self-efficacy can be increased by:

- ✔ Linking a new project to a recent success. For example, knowing that you can achieve something because it is very similar to your last project.

- ✔ Being offered encouragement to build up confidence. For example, hearing someone say, 'I know you'll succeed and I have every confidence that you can do this'.

- ✔ Providing a role model or peer support. Take time to consider how your role model would act and what they would say or do in this situation.

- ✔ Suggesting new or alternative ways of achieving a goal. For example, saying to yourself 'I know I am good at doing this my way'. Accept that your approach is fine, even though it could be different from what other people suggest.

- ✔ Experiencing success – success raises self-efficacy. Remind yourself that you've been successful before and can be successful again.

- ✔ Knowing how to deal with your response to stressful situations. In a stressful situation the way a person responds can markedly alter their self-efficacy. For example, a person with low self-efficacy who gets nervous speaking in front of an audience can take this as a sign of their lack of ability for public speaking, thus lowering their self-efficacy further. In contrast, a person with high self-efficacy is likely to interpret feeling nervous as quite normal and unrelated to his or her actual ability. It is the person's concern about the _implications_ of their physiological response that alters their self-efficacy, rather than the response itself.

Taking control of your mind

Understanding how self-efficacy affects the way you control your mind can help you decide how to move forward.

- ✔ **Making choices:** You are more inclined to take on tasks if you believe you can succeed and have high self-efficacy. If your self-efficacy leads you to overestimate your ability to take on and complete a task, you may have problems!

  To achieve your goal and get the result you want, your level of self-efficacy needs to be a little above your ability, encouraging you to tackle challenging tasks and so gain valuable experience.

- ✔ **Motivation:** If you have high self-efficacy when carrying out a task you are more likely to put in more effort and stay motivated than if you have low self-efficacy. However, having low self-efficacy can give you the incentive to find out more about the subject and up your skills. Alternatively, if you enjoy high self-efficacy you need to ask yourself whether you have done your homework before taking on the task.

- ✔ **Your thought patterns and responses:** Low self-efficacy can lead you to believe a task is harder than it actually is. This often results in making the task harder than it need be as well as increasing stress. Having high self-efficacy means you take a wider view of a task to assess what you need to do next. People with high self-efficacy aren't daunted by obstacles but find ways of overcoming them. A person with a high self-efficacy attributes failure to external factors, whereas a person with low self-efficacy attributes failure to low ability. For example, a person with high self-efficacy may attribute a poor result in their French exam to external factors such as a harder than usual test. A person with a low self-efficacy attributes a poor result to their lack of ability for learning languages.

- ✔ **Controlling your destiny:** Bandura showed that people with high self-efficacy (confidence) or low self-efficacy view the world in fundamentally different ways. People with a high self-efficacy (confidence) generally believe they are in control of their own lives, while people with low self-efficacy blame themselves if something goes wrong.

Struggling to Maintain Motivation

Sometimes you can find yourself struggling to maintain your motivation. Knowing something about psychological theories concerning motivation can help you get a handle on why you feel the way you do.

Finding your inner strength

The following theories may shed some light on ways of finding your inner strength and keeping yourself motivated.

The Expectancy Theory

Following on from Maslow, Victor Vroom created his 'Expectancy Theory' in 1964. Vroom attempts to explain why people follow certain courses of action in the workplace. He introduced three variables, affecting how you feel and how you perform: value, expectancy, and instrumentality.

- *Value* is the importance you place on the expected outcome of a situation.

- *Expectancy* is the belief that your output and the success of the situation are linked: for example, by working harder, your situation improves.

- *Instrumentality* is the belief that the success of the situation is linked to the expected outcome of the situation: for example, the project has gone really well and you are expecting praise.

Vroom came up with an equation summing up the three different aspects affecting motivation. The equation explains motivation from the perspective of why people choose to follow a particular course of action:

Motivation = perceived probability of success (expectancy) × connection of success and reward (instrumentality) × value of obtaining goals (value)

For example, you apply for a new job believing that you'll be offered the position, that the increased salary is worth having, and that the job will satisfy your goal of moving up the career ladder. All these elements need to be in place for you to be successful with your job application.

Vroom proposes that a low value in one area (for example, value of obtaining goals) results in a low value of motivation. All three factors have to be present for motivation to occur. If all three factors aren't present, the probability is low that you're going to engage in any new learning or new behaviour, and you're likely to struggle to maintain your motivation. For example:

- By *not* believing you can be successful

- By *not* seeing a connection between your input and your success

- By *not* valuing the results of your success

Someone needing to lose weight has to believe they can actually do it, that by eating less and exercising more they will achieve their goal, and that their improved image and enhanced health will be worth the effort.

Vroom believes that how motivated you are depends on whether you want a reward for doing a good job and whether you believe making more effort leads to that reward. His Expectancy Theory can apply to any situation where someone does something because they expect a particular outcome.

Take the example of recycling:

- ✔ You recycle as much as you can because you think it's important to conserve resources and you're taking a stand on environmental issues (value).

- ✔ You think that the more effort you put into recycling, the more household and workplace items you can recycle (expectancy).

- ✔ You think that the more items you recycle, the lower the effect on the environment (instrumentality).

Vroom's Expectancy Theory is about the connections a person can make towards an expected outcome and how much he or she can contribute to the outcome. In the workplace, the Expectancy Theory is used in the belief that employee effort leads to performance and performance leads to rewards. Rewards may be positive or negative. The more positive the reward, the more likely the employee is going to be highly motivated. Conversely, the more negative the reward, the less likely the employee is going to maintain their motivation.

Modern theories

In 2001 Nohria, Lawrence, and Wilson put forward the theory that in the world of work, you are influenced and guided by four basic drives: acquiring, bonding, learning, defending. Paying attention to the four drives can help you find and maintain your inner strength:

- ✔ Acquiring goods and life experiences helps in driving you forward.

- ✔ Creating a bond of mutual care and commitment with others helps you to feel good about yourself.

- ✔ Actively seeking enlightenment helps you to make sense of the world and your reason for being.

- ✔ Defending yourself, your loved ones, your beliefs, and what you own from harm.

If your four basic needs are met, finding your inner strength and knowing what you want or where you're going in life are easier. If any of the basic needs are missing, finding the strength inside yourself to motivate yourself to achieve your goals is much harder.

Overcoming the barriers

Barriers stop you from achieving what you want to achieve. Taking time to understand the root cause of the barrier pays dividends in the long run. Some of the barriers you come up against can be to do with addressing your intrinsic and extrinsic needs.

Understanding intrinsic and extrinsic motivation

To help you overcome your barriers, applying internal values (intrinsic) and external factors (extrinsic) to the situation can help you regain your motivation. (Chapter 6 tells you about being internally and externally referenced.) Table 2-2 shows how teachers set about boosting the motivation of their students through internal values and external factors.

Table 2-2	Boosting Student Motivation
Intrinsic Motivation of Students (encouraging motivation through internal values)	**Extrinsic Motivation of Students (motivation coming from external factors)**
Explaining why acquiring skills and knowledge is important	Listing clear expectations
Creating or maintaining curiosity	Giving positive feedback
Using a variety of activities, games, and aids (using all the senses) to stimulate learning	Providing rewards
	Publicly acknowledging success
Using simulations to encourage students to come up with their own ideas	Setting detailed guidelines
Encouraging students to set their own learning goals	Emphasising the importance of good grades
Relating learning to student needs	Offering awards for outstanding work
Helping students develop their own plan of action	

Teachers need to emphasise the importance of the intrinsic values to their students while recognising that some intrinsic values may not be right for some students. The extrinsic suggestions work, but only as long as the student is under the control of the teacher. Outside the classroom, unless the student has internalised the desired goals and behaviours, he soon drops the desired behaviour and operates according to his internal standards or other external factors.

Considering basic human needs

In 2001, The Institute for Management Excellence suggested nine basic human needs to maintain motivation and overcome barriers:

- Security
- Adventure
- Freedom
- Exchange
- Power
- Expansion
- Acceptance
- Community
- Expression

After an employee's basic needs are met, motivation doesn't cost the employer anything, except for time and effort. The following views adapted (with permission) from Fenman Ltd (2003) can give you ideas for overcoming barriers:

- Meeting basic needs costs money – salary or wages
- Motivators don't always cost money, for example: praising, talking, listening
- Treating employees well – but finding out first *how* they like to be treated
- Considering the best way of keeping employees motivated
- Treating each person as an individual
- Discussing approaches to getting motivated with each individual employee

✔ Developing practical approaches to workloads

✔ Praising good work

✔ Encouraging progress

✔ Listening to your team members

✔ Showing you care by spending time with your employees

Putting the above ideas into practice in the workplace or at home can help you take a more positive approach to achieving your goals, avoiding some of the barriers, and helping to keep you motivated.

Chapter 3

Preparing Yourself for Motivation

· ·

In This Chapter

▶ Figuring out what you want to tackle first

▶ Gearing up to take action

▶ Setting the scene for success

· ·

*G*etting yourself motivated to take on a task isn't always easy. You can find yourself stumbling before even arriving at the starting line. In this chapter, I help you to identify your priorities so you can commit to that first action and then move forward confidently with your chosen project.

Identifying Your Priorities

Identifying your priorities involves taking stock of your home and work life and deciding where you need to make changes. Pressure of work or demands to complete a particular task – for example, a project with a deadline, an exam, or a family party – may decide your priorities for you.

Taking the time to decide your priorities by looking at deadlines can propel you into action; otherwise you may be tempted to just do the tasks you like most of all, and not necessarily the most important ones!

You can also take a look at Chapter 5 where I talk about goal setting to help you focus on your key goals and achievable tasks.

If you find yourself overwhelmed with priorities, don't panic! The first step in prioritising your goals is to identify the key areas for you; for example, aspects of your work, home, or family. Your priority may be just one or several of these areas. Writing down your priorities is a start in itself because it allows your mind to start preparing for action.

Table 3-1 lists examples of home and work tasks that may be on your task list. Use Table 3-2 to create your own list of priorities.

Table 3-1	Identifying Your Tasks
Home Tasks	*Work Tasks*
Preparing for a party or celebration	Completing a project
Clearing out old clothes	Writing a report
Reorganising drawers, cupboards, or rooms	Arranging a meeting
Reviewing finances and paying household bills	Applying for an award
Examining household insurance contracts	Writing a presentation or paper
Decorating a room	Preparing your 5-year company plan
Weeding the garden, mowing the lawn, preparing a flower bed	Planning new advertising literature
Tidying the garden shed	Following up on sales leads
Writing a personal letter	Arranging a team event or away day
Filing away home documents	Preparing for a proposal or tender submission

Table 3-2	My Personal Task List
Home Tasks	*Work Tasks*

Just writing your list of home and work tasks means that you are starting to take action.

Starting with the end in sight

The stimulus for getting motivated often varies from person to person. Having an idea of what your completed task may look, feel, or sound like helps to move the project forward. For some of you, just the thought of being able to get your clothes back in the cupboard or enjoying a newly decorated room gives you an incentive.

For others, the motivation may come from a completely different source. For example, some time ago, a friend was in despair over her teenage son's bedroom, which looked like a bombsite. She couldn't get into the room for piles of clothes everywhere, CDs littering the floor, and general chaos. Several months later when I was visiting my friend, I was delighted to hear that the teenager had finally tidied up his room. When I asked my friend's son what had motivated him, he said it was because he simply couldn't stand his mother's nagging any longer!

Knowing what you want to achieve allows your unconscious mind to start working for you and lets your brain start processing the steps you need to take.

Be realistic about your goal to make sure that you don't fall at the first hurdle. Choosing to clear one cupboard or drawer is more realistic than deciding to sort out the whole room. Writing the key headings for a presentation is more realistic than trying to write the whole presentation in one go.

Cutting up what you are trying to achieve into bitesize chunks makes your task easier and helps you to feel more motivated.

Think about one of your priorities and imagine having completed the task. Use your senses of seeing, hearing, and feeling to imagine how your finished project looks now and enjoy the sense of achievement from having completed the task.

Highlighting what matters to you

The decision about what matters most may be forced on you if you're facing a deadline, financial penalty, or loss of a contract. Think about which of the following areas applies to your priorities and then write down your top three priorities:

- ✔ Avoiding a financial penalty by completing the task by a certain date
- ✔ Keeping to an agreed date for the submission of a project
- ✔ Being aware that other people are relying on your input
- ✔ Having the time to do something you enjoy after completing your project
- ✔ Choosing the priority that best helps your promotional prospects
- ✔ Earning a bonus
- ✔ Completing the priority is likely to have a positive impact on your health

If you don't have a priority dictated to you by the preceding list, then think about the following questions:

- ✔ Which goal is the most important to me?
- ✔ Which one will give me the most satisfaction when I achieve it?
- ✔ Which goal has the most pressing deadline attached to it?

Work out whether you're motivated by tasks which are easy to do and that give you high satisfaction or tasks that give low satisfaction, yet which are still very important, such as filing or paying bills.

Getting Yourself Ready

After deciding which task to start first (see the preceding section), and having made sure you have the skills or abilities to achieve the task, you can think about when and where to start. At this stage, beware of being side-tracked. Suddenly, cutting the grass, going to lunch, and reading emails may have more appeal than the task at hand! Rather than tackling the big project immediately, you may find doing activities that sidetrack you to be easier and feel like you're actually doing something important. In fact you're just using delaying tactics! The enormity of the task at hand and the anxiety you feel can delay you getting started.

I often find that I need to allow myself half an hour to deal with a few small tasks before starting work on my main priority. These tasks can include checking that no emails need my immediate attention, or making a phone call. After dealing with these things, my mind is then clear to focus on the main task at hand.

Choosing a start date

Imagine that you're preparing for an evening out with friends. Your preparations take into account what time you're meeting at the restaurant and how long it's going to take you to shower, change, and travel to the venue. Likewise, choosing when to start your project is the same as getting ready for an evening out – it involves planning and scheduling.

Ask yourself the following questions:

- ✔ Where's your project going to take you?
- ✔ Who's going to be involved?

✔ Why's your project important?

✔ What's the timescale?

✔ When are you planning to start?

Start with one of the easier elements of your task. This way you avoid inventing hurdles and delaying your start. For example, when writing this book, rather than tackling one of the larger chapters first, I began with some of the smaller sections first so that I felt I'd made a start.

To ensure that you don't set yourself up for failure from the start, consider the following examples of sensible planning:

✔ If you're not a morning person, don't plan to exercise in the morning.

✔ If you need the space around you to be tidy before you feel able to tackle your project, allow yourself some time to tidy the room where you work. If you don't do this first, you'll continue to be distracted by things around you.

✔ If you're looking after your 2-year-old niece, don't plan to reorganise your entire filing system while she's with you.

✔ If you know that straight after lunch is your least energetic time of day, don't plan to start a task then.

Committing to the first action

Committing to taking your first action includes the following:

✔ Finding a day, time, and place to start

✔ Setting the start date

✔ Telling your family and friends, if appropriate, so that they don't plan something else for you at the same time

✔ Creating a space around you so that you can work comfortably

Committing to the first action helps you to move forward and away from the 'stuck' state.

Creating a Motivational Environment

Your environment can impact powerfully on your motivation. What's going on around you may not be immediately obvious but can still have an impact on getting you started and having a clear focus.

Take a moment to look around you. What can you see and hear? For example, do you need your environment to be quiet and peaceful and free from distractions so that you're in the right frame of mind to read this book?

It's easy to underestimate the importance of your environment and the impact it can have on your energy or enthusiasm to tackle tasks. This section helps you to evaluate your environment (both the seen and unseen) to see if it helps you, or where simple changes could make a real difference. Take the example of someone who piles papers up under their desk to ensure their desk area is clear. Unfortunately, the effect of the pile of papers will still be distracting!

Evaluating your environment

Think about the following aspects of your environment to create the best setting for you:

- **Lighting:** Do you have natural daylight in your work area? Does the sunlight glare on your computer screen? Is the lighting in the right position and good enough for you to work efficiently?

- **Sound:** Do you need quiet or do you prefer working with background noise – people talking, planes flying overhead, busy traffic? Some people can work well with background noise or music playing. Others are distracted by the slightest sound.

- **Space and view:** Do you have enough space to work comfortably? Is your in-tray overflowing, papers piling up on all sides, or is stuff crammed under your desk or behind your working area? What view do you have from your window or your office area? Does what you see motivate or distract you?

- **Colour:** What colour are the walls painted and are there pictures on the walls to brighten up your surroundings? Is the scene uplifting and stimulating or grey and uninspiring?

- **Seating:** Is your chair comfortable or too comfortable? Is it ergonomically designed to support your back and helping you to maintain a good posture? Is your chair at the right height so you can work at your computer with your hands at the correct level for your keyboard? Do you need a footstool to keep your back in the correct position?

✔ **Equipment:** Do you have all the equipment you need to use regularly at hand, for example, computer, copier, paper, pens, and pencils?

✔ **Fresh air:** Can you open the windows to let fresh air into your office? Or, if your office windows aren't designed to open or you work in a basement office, do you have air-conditioning?

✔ **Temperature:** Are you in a room with a controlled temperature or can you adjust the thermostat to make the room warmer or cooler?

Fill in Table 3-3 to find out how your environment is affecting you.

Table 3-3	My Working Environment	
Key Aspect of My Environment	**What I Have Around Me**	**Score Each Area** **1 to 10** **1 = poor** **10 = excellent**
Lighting		
Sound		
Space and view		
Colour		
Seating		
Equipment		
Fresh air		
Temperature		

Look at the areas with the lowest scores to see how you can make some simple changes to improve those areas.

Motivating music

Different kinds of music can inspire and stimulate. Is there a certain tune or song that motivates you to get started and keep moving? When I am writing, I always have my favourite classical music playing quietly in the background. It helps me to focus and keeps me feeling motivated.

The number of people listening to music while exercising has also increased dramatically. Gyms and health clubs often play music with a strong rhythm to encourage and motivate people to stick with their exercise plan.

Don G. Campbell has explored the effect of music on the brain in *The Mozart Effect*. Music stimulates brainwaves or patterns inducing different states within the body. The brainwave is similar to a heart beat, and differs in frequency dependent on the tempo and pace of the music.

ANECDOTE

Motivating myself to write

After I agreed to write this book, I had to get motivated to start. My first action was to clear time in my diary for this project. I noted my writing sessions in my diary as appointments, cancelling other commitments, so I could get on with my writing. I told my family and friends that I was writing a book in the hope that they wouldn't try to disturb or distract me.

To motivate myself, I set a deadline for each chapter, and scheduled review stages with editors and colleagues to keep me on track. I knew how important the task was for me and the satisfaction writing the book would give me. I imagined what each finished chapter looked like and how I would feel when I had the first draft prepared and emailed to my editor.

I took regular short breaks for fresh air and exercise and took care to eat the right foods to help my brain function well and drank plenty of water to keep hydrated.

To reach my goal, I broke each chapter into manageable sections so I felt a sense of achievement at the completion of each section. The breaks gave my brain time to process what I had written and to help me decide where I needed to make changes or add information.

I am motivated to write early in the morning, benefiting from the daylight (and even sunshine!) and I have a stimulating view from my writing area. Before starting to write, I cleaned and tidied my work area so I could focus on the project without any unwanted distractions. And I got into the habit of returning phone calls, dealing with emails, and other tasks after I finished my writing for the day.

There are four brain states creating four different brain patterns:

- ✔ **Beta state**: The beta state is brought about by fast, lively, loud music, often more than 80 beats a minute (the sort of music your teenagers may be playing!). Beta music is good to listen to if you have a tendency to drop off after lunch. This is the type of music to keep you alert, active, and working. Mozart's *Marriage of Figaro* is a good example of fast moving and lively music.

- ✔ **Alpha state:** The alpha state is reached by listening to slower music at around 60 to 80 beats a minute, such as Bach, Beethoven, Handel, or Mozart. This type of music encourages the brain to send out brainwaves of a similar pace to the music, thus helping the brain in concentrating and focusing on a task. Being in an alpha state also assists memory and creativity and is sometimes described as a state of relaxed attentiveness. Alpha state music also encourages stimulation and cross over between the right and left sides of the brain.

- ✔ **Theta state**: Theta state music is the type of music you hear while having a massage treatment. Being in the theta state can make you feel very sleepy.

- ✔ **Delta state:** Delta state music can put you into a trance. It's frequently used for meditating and can send you into a deep sleep.

To enhance your motivation, stay with alpha or beta music because the slower music of the theta and delta states is unlikely to get you moving!

Setting up a supportive network

A supportive network of family, friends, work colleagues, or business partners can have a powerful influence on how well you're motivated. Although you may be reluctant to ask for help, finding support is an important step in motivating yourself to meet your goals.

To help prepare yourself for motivation, find the time to talk about your project with those who support you. Talking helps you clarify which areas of the project or task are really important.

A problem shared is a problem halved.

Part II
Identifying and Maintaining Change

'The motivation to be a lion tamer came from his years as an inner-city school teacher.'

In this part. . .

Sometimes setbacks and fear can get in the way of your motivation. Here you discover how to summon up your motivation to overcome barriers and make changes to keep you moving forward. You also find out how to face up to your demons and what steps to take to hold on firmly to your end goal. Exploring the technique of visualisation also helps to propel you into action as you travel through time, keeping your end goal in view.

Chapter 4

Summoning the Motivation to Change

*Y*ou want to make changes to improve your quality of life but find yourself facing a brick wall. So, how do you get yourself motivated to achieve what is closest to your heart? In this chapter, you find out how to overcome all those barriers and excuses that stop you bringing about change, while at the same time discovering the agent that propels you into action.

Finding a Catalyst for Change

Think about buying that new suit. Do you have a particular reason for needing a new suit: a function, job interview, or just to impress your new girlfriend? The event defines the time and place when you need the new suit. Taking action involves deciding when you go shopping, which shops to visit, whether you need a friend to help, the kind of suit you want, and how much you can afford to spend.

Likewise, planning to take action involves a reason, need, or a deadline. In many cases your action can be linked to a catalyst – something or someone that catapults you into action. The catalyst may be negative or positive, or pushing you toward or away from something.

Catalysts can come in different shapes and sizes:

- ✔ Take Ron, for example. When he went to see his doctor for a routine blood pressure (BP) test, Ron found that his BP was on the high side, but immediately decided he didn't want to take medication to get his BP down. As an alternative the doctor suggested a change of diet and exercise as a way of helping to reduce Ron's BP.

  The catalyst spurring Ron into action was his concern about having to take medication to lower his BP. He immediately embarked on a plan of regular exercise, walking every day for at least 40 to 60 minutes. Ron realised that because of work commitments he'd been getting less exercise, had gained weight, and wasn't as fit and healthy as he used to be. Ron took the action of reducing his BP into his own hands by avoiding medication and adopting a new exercise regime.

- ✔ Susie was advised by her dentist to floss her teeth every day. This habit was new for Susie and she felt she didn't have the time for daily flossing – or so she thought! However, Susie regularly applied eye-cream and moisturiser. Surprisingly, what motivated Susie to get flossing came hidden in her eye-cream. She'd recently changed to a new brand, which needed a few minutes to absorb into her skin. Those few minutes were all she needed to give herself time to floss her teeth, and hey presto, Susie's time barrier vanished. The catalyst for change was imposed on Susie simply by her innocently purchasing a new product.

To help you with your plan of action, consider which of the following apply to you:

- ✔ You're only going to do the task if it's easy.
- ✔ You need to make time to start.
- ✔ You need the impetus of a deadline.
- ✔ You want to feel positive about the task.
- ✔ You want to see a positive outcome.
- ✔ You can afford the costs involved.
- ✔ You have the right skills.

Taking Your First Steps

Committing to taking your first step to action isn't always easy. It can involve overcoming excuses, barriers, and delays, frequently of your own making!

For some people the action of opening the diary or electronic organiser, or even finding some paper to write a 'to do' list, is an important first step as this helps you to organise and clarify tasks. Taking time to write notes down can help identify the key areas, and a diary provides some structure to plan activities and makes finding the time to begin them easier to do, providing you write them into the diary with realistic timescales beside each task.

Here are a couple of examples of first steps:

✔ Three friends were carrying out major renovations on an old building, which involved demolition work. They decided that the first and most important step of their action plan was a trip to the DIY store to buy protective clothing because they knew that the work was going to be dirty, dusty, and possibly dangerous. Their next step was booking a skip from the local council. Finally a time was fixed to do the actual demolition work. But health and safety came first.

✔ A colleague wanted to create more space in her small home office to make working easier and grow her business. Her first major step was to arrange for a friend to coordinate the office move so that she could carry on with running her business during the refurbishment process. The friend moved her computer and filing cabinet to another room so that she could carry on her business while the room was being refurbished. The friend took the old furniture to a charity shop, co-ordinated ordering new fitted furniture, and employed a plasterer to repair the walls where the old furniture had stood. My colleague was motivated throughout the upheaval by the knowledge that her newly designed office would allow her to expand her business. Just as importantly, she didn't lose valuable clients during the disruption and refurbishment.

Look at the following list of first steps and decide which are most important to you:

✔ Making a list of important jobs you need to do

✔ Tidying your desk so you can start working on a project

✔ Blocking out time in your diary for your task

✔ Spending time researching a new course on the Internet

✔ Asking friends for advice or recommendations, such as the name of a cleaning agency, virtual assistant, or computer specialist, for example

✔ Taking a break or exercise

✔ Cleaning and tidying your work area to improve efficiency

✔ Sorting your in-tray and prioritising urgent tasks

Taking the first steps is important. However, starting in the right place, or, in other words, planning the project so that you take the right first steps, is essential. For example, when clearing your garage, attic, or spare room, your first step is to make sure you have enough black sacks or recycling boxes to store the items you plan to keep. It can be quite demotivating to discover, if you don't have a system in place, that after all your hard work you have little idea of what to keep and what to throw out. If you plan your clear out efficiently, you don't end up putting back what you fully intended taking to the charity shop or the council dump.

Some people need to have a cup of tea or coffee in their hand before they can take action. Decide if you're one of those people and get the kettle on to make your cup of tea straight away so you can take your first step!

Discovering Values That Motivate

Values are your belief system. They help you evaluate and interpret what is important to you, acting like a filter. Values are the things in life that really matter to you, that are generally worth having, and that drive your thinking and behaviour. The values you cherish can affect the choices you make about friends, career decisions, or how you spend your leisure time. Your upbringing, family and friends, perhaps the newspapers you read play a large part in confirming your values. Although your values frequently act as powerful motivators, they can also have the effect of demotivating you.

To discover the values that motivate you look at the list in Table 4-1. Be aware of what you feel as you read each word and mark the values that are important to you.

Table 4-1		Highlighting Your Values	
Value	*Important*	*Value*	*Important*
Integrity		Empathy	
Loyalty		Trustworthiness	
Honesty		Orderliness	
Caring		Disciplined	
Openness		Diplomatic	
Appreciativeness		Tactfulness	
Friendliness		Sincerity	
Responsible		Independence	
Supportive		Honourableness	
Politeness		Punctuality	
Fairness		Faithfulness	

The values you hold can impact your motivation. Generally, motivation only happens if your chosen values are being upheld by your actions. Your values need to be in line and not conflict with your actions. For example:

- ✔ If you hold *friendliness* and *politeness* as important values, you find that improving customer service goes hand in hand with these values.

- ✔ Valuing *appreciativeness* motivates you to always thank someone for the good work they've done. Or, you may well be motivated to work even harder for clients who express their appreciation.

If you find yourself having difficulty summoning the motivation to do something, it's sometimes because the task clashes with your values. For example, you care strongly about honesty and integrity. You are asked by management to source the cheapest products for a meal, and then told you must charge the customers a premium price. It is likely that you feel thoroughly demotivated and unwilling to carry out the task.

Honouring your values increases your motivation to carry out your actions.

For example, the manager of a nursing home arranged for all the team to attend sales training. One member of staff kept cancelling the training (for valid reasons). When questioned she said she was a *nurse* and not a 'sales person'. Her job was *caring* and she felt the sales training would violate her strongly held value. She eventually attended the sales training after the trainer helped her to see that this extra training enhanced her caring by making it possible to offer more services to her clients. Because her values were now in line with the training, she was more than happy to take part.

Recognising Your Roadblocks

Knowing what causes you to feel demotivated and stops you taking action is vital to the success of your action plan. Even though facing up to the culprit can be painful!

Perhaps you're demotivated from starting the task you have set yourself because you have so many other essential jobs that must be done first: taking the children to school, feeding the cat, walking the dog.

One helpful technique is to make sure that you *do not set yourself up to fail*. Choose a realistic time to start your task, allowing yourself enough time to do the other 'must do' jobs first.

Identifying your demotivators

Do you recognise any of the following demotivators preventing you from getting into action?

- ✔ The task doesn't tie in with what you want to achieve.
- ✔ You don't have a positive gut instinct about the task.
- ✔ You feel overwhelmed.
- ✔ The task just doesn't look right for you.
- ✔ You don't have the time.
- ✔ You can't afford to finance the task.
- ✔ You don't see yourself benefiting from the task.
- ✔ You're scared to pick up the phone and commit.
- ✔ You have too many other priorities.
- ✔ The deadline is too tight for you.

Acknowledging your excuses

When summoning the motivation to change, it's okay to admit to having excuses. Identifying an excuse can help you to overcome a barrier to action. As you acknowledge the excuse, consider what effect the excuse is having on your planned task. Is the excuse genuine, is it there just to put you off taking action, is there a deeper reason behind the excuse? Taking time to consider that your excuses can help you view the action required in a different way allows you to tackle the task differently.

A friend wanted to update her working practices by listing her new contacts on a database and sending information to them using printed address labels. But she claimed that she couldn't find a software package that was compatible with her present computer. Having spoken to several software specialists she said that they were unable to solve the problem. Her excuse was that whatever software was available, it wasn't easy to use. Her excuse of being *easy to use* was very important to her, so she continued to use her old system of writing address labels by hand. With a friend's help and a more open mind, she eventually worked out an easy way to use her existing software system to prevent her having to hand write labels in the future. Her original block was eventually overcome by allowing herself to be open-minded and to tackle her fear of technology.

Here are a few common excuses you may readily recognise and some positive actions to help the person move forward:

- ✔ I don't have enough time – but I could get up 30 minutes earlier to give me the time I need

- ✔ I can't afford it – but if I started saving a small amount each month, I would eventually be able to

- ✔ I don't have the skills – but I could go to evening class and gain new skills

- ✔ I've never done this before – but I could ask a colleague who's familiar with the issue

- ✔ I don't know who to ask – but I could ask around for recommendations

- ✔ I'm scared of the consequences – but the consequences of not doing anything are just as bad

Making Use of the Positive By-Products

Positive by-product is a term for the benefits you get by *not* taking action. So why *not*? Because the positive by-product can turn out to be your best course of action.

You may eventually decide not to do something so that you don't change a current situation. Consider the following examples:

- ✔ You decide not to move house to stay near your friends and avoid going through the process of having to meet new people.

- ✔ You decide not to lose so much weight, so you don't need to overcome being shy.

- ✔ You decide not to buy a new outfit, so you can save some money for a house project that you realise is more important to you.

- ✔ You decide not to apply for a new job, so you can stay where you feel comfortable and don't have to cope with change, upheaval, and learning new skills.

The positive by-product varies from person to person and is often hidden in your subconscious.

To summon your motivation to change, it is important to know if there is a positive by-product to be gained by *not* taking the action. It is likely that you have a very good reason for not doing what you set down in your action plan.

Taking time to consider why you're sitting on the fence and not pursuing your goal can be worthwhile. Identifying what's stopping you achieving is key to summoning your motivation. The positive by-product can be preventing you from taking action. For example, if the price of promotion means spending less time with your family and interfering with your leisure time, you may well come up with good reasons why you don't want to apply for the promotion that you've been telling yourself you really want! Staying in a comfortable job that leaves plenty of time for spending with family and for leisure may be more important than the perceived benefits of the promotion.

A woman had mountains of ironing to do but she simply couldn't face it. She admitted to herself that her real reason wasn't the ironing itself but the spiders lurking in the cupboard where the ironing board was stored! Her fear of spiders was stopping her getting on with the job. Once her husband had got rid of the spiders she had no problem keeping on top of the ironing. The positive by-product of *not* doing the ironing was not confronting her fear of spiders. You could argue that she had an additional by-product of keeping her husband around when she ironed, so he knew how hard she worked at home. If she got over her fear of the spiders, her husband could go out and leave her to iron whenever he wanted!

Chapter 5

Goal Setting

· ·

· ·

Goal setting is a great way of helping you to achieve an ambition in any area of your life. You can set yourself a goal to help you accomplish anything from the smallest task to a major project, covering vastly different timescales, and your goal can be purely private or involve a lot of people. And remember you can set goals at any time, not just at New Year!

Knowing how to set goals effectively helps you to bring about the desired changes in your life. In this chapter, you discover how to define your goal, highlight your key priorities, and plan a strategy to help achieve them. You also find out how to break your goal down into manageable chunks and how to identify and avoid those obstacles that can get in the way of your success.

Defining Your Goals

Getting motivated to achieve your goal plays a big part in the success of your enterprise. Motivation can be enhanced by making sure that your goal is clearly defined. Here are some tips to help you define your goal:

- ✔ **State the goal in the positive.** What do I want? What is that going to do for me? For example: 'My goal is to attend the gym every Monday,' not 'My goal is to stop being fat.'

- ✔ **Define the context of your goal.** When, where, and with who do you want to achieve your goal? Are other people linked to your goal?

- ✔ **Write down your goal.** Writing allows you to redefine your goal and make it more specific, fixing your goal firmly in your consciousness.

- ✔ **Make sure you have the necessary skills.** You need to be able to start and keep up the actions needed to achieve your goal. Do you need to buy in or get skills or resources from other people?

✔ **Do you have the time, money, and energy to achieve your goal?** Does your goal fit in with your purpose in life?

✔ **Be aware of any positive by-products of not achieving your goal.** (Refer to Chapter 4.) If there are positive by-products think about how you can achieve them in another way.

✔ **Be ready to start.** Do you have all the tools and equipment to hand that you will need to get going?

✔ **Maintain a positive state of mind about your goal.** If you have just been battling with your bank manager, you may not be in the right state of mind to define your goal!

✔ **Imagine your success.** Keep the enjoyment about the achievement of your goal uppermost in your mind.

✔ **Visualise your goal.** Picture what you will see, what you will hear, and what you will feel when you achieve your goal, using all your senses as I describe in Chapter 6.

Applying the SMART rule

SMART is an acronym for 'Specific, Measurable, Achievable, Realistic, Timescale' and is a tool commonly used in business for setting goals. You too can use the SMART principles to great effect when setting a goal, helping you structure and define your goal clearly and accurately.

Tackling New Year's resolutions

It is 1 January and you announce to your friends that your New Year's resolution is to join a gym. Feeling motivated you sign up the next day at the local gym, pay the joining fee, and arrange the monthly direct debit for the annual membership. Come 1 February you realise you have only been to the gym once and you don't feel motivated to go again – what has gone wrong?

The answer is quite simple. Your publicly stated goal of joining the gym has been achieved. But it wasn't actually the goal you wanted to achieve! The goal you wanted to achieve was probably losing weight, dropping a dress size, or getting fit.

To stand a chance of attaining your goal, you need to define the goal carefully and precisely. In this example, 'joining the gym' was just one step towards achieving the goal of becoming fit. It was not the goal in itself. No wonder the true goal wasn't achieved. It is impossible to aim for a goal that has not yet been defined.

On a side note, you can set goals at any time. However, New Year does provide a fresh start, a clean slate, a new beginning. And if you miss New Year, you can always choose Chinese New Year instead!

Write down your goal and, using SMART, defin
expand your description to include the SMAR

- ✔ **S**pecific: Describe precisely what you wa
  going to do, how you are going to do it, an
  Make sure you state your intentions clearl
  a French tuition class because my goal is t
  speak French during my summer holiday.'

- ✔ **M**easurable: It is important to be able to mea
  how you're getting on, can see change occurr
  know when your goal has been achieved. For example: 'My goal is to
  learn enough French to be able to buy things in the market, order food
  in a restaurant, and ask directions if I get lost.'

- ✔ **A**chievable or **a**ttainable: Goals need to be within your reach so that you
  can achieve them and commit to them. However, your goal also needs
  to stretch your skills. If your goal is too easy the commitment may not
  be strong enough to keep you motivated. For example: 'My goal is to use
  the ability I already have to learn enough French to enhance my holiday,
  and to commit to attending French classes.'

- ✔ **R**ealistic: Is your goal realistic with the resources and tools available to
  you? For example, can you find a good teacher with whom you will be
  able to learn enough French in the three months available to you.

- ✔ **T**imescale, **t**imely: Make sure that you set a timescale for your goal: for
  example, by your birthday, next week, next month, by the end of the year.
  Your timescale provides a clear parameter in which to work. It also gives
  you a baseline to start from. Your timescale, like your goal, must be realistic, measurable, and achievable. For example: 'My goal is to attend weekly
  French classes for three months, starting in two weeks' time.'

Once you have set SMART goals you can make them even SMART**ER**.

- ✔ **E**xpand your goal: Add in more detail to see where you need to put in
  extra effort. For example: 'I'm arranging to meet my French friend and
  am going to ask her to speak to me in French.'

- ✔ **R**eview regularly: Check how you are progressing. How are you getting
  on with your French tuition? Do you need to spend more time practising
  at home or listening to spoken French on a CD or DVD in the car while
  travelling?

To see an example of the SMART model in action, see the sidebar 'Getting
SMART' on the next page.

Taking steps to action

You've defined your goal precisely (see preceding section), but you may not necessarily know which step to take first in achieving your goal! Figure 5-1 takes you through a 5-step process to identify the first step you need to take.

In Figure 5-1, the numbers in the circles are placed in a different order from the usual 1, 2, 3, 4, 5 sequence. This order is very important for the process. Draw five circles and number each one as shown. As you progress through the following steps, write down each answer in the appropriate circle in the order shown.

1. Define your goal.

Step 1 is your goal of cleaning the car. Write this goal in the number 1 circle, to the far right, as shown.

Getting SMART

A friend had a goal of becoming fitter after giving birth to her first child. To keep motivated she arranged to take part in a fun run with some other new mums. She worked out that they could all meet weekly for coffee and a walk. Each week three mums would go out for a short brisk walk or mini jog whilst the remaining three looked after the six babies. When the first group returned, the mums would swap roles. In that way over a period of just over an hour, all the mums would have time for some exercise and a cup of coffee, with the babies being looked after. A weekly commitment would help them achieve their overall goal of competing in the local 5-kilometre fun run in 8 weeks' time.

Using the SMART model, my friend defined her goal as follows:

S – My goal is to feel fit enough to run the 5-kilometre fun run in 8 weeks' time.

M – My goal is to complete the 5-kilometre circuit and feel OK at the end!

A – My goal is to meet with a group of mums each week to share the babysitting and have

the opportunity for some exercise at the same time.

R – My goal is to increase my fitness through brisk walking and jogging over an 8-week period.

T – My goal is to meet with the five other mums every week and jog with them for 20–30 minutes over a period of 8 weeks.

My friend also incorporated some of the SMART**ER** principles.

E – She arranged to do some exercise herself in between the weekly sessions. This was made up of brisk walks and an occasional run when her husband was able to help with child care.

R – She reviewed her progress regularly and reported back to tell me how she was getting on.

My friend completed the fun run and enjoyed the day in difficult weather conditions. On the day of the fun run, her husband unexpectedly had to work so she arranged for a friend to look after her daughter while she took part in the fun run.

Figure 5-1:
Follow this
process
to figure
out your
first step in
achieving
your goal.

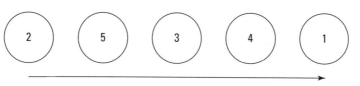

2. **Describe where you are now.**

   Step 2 is describing where you are now – you have a very dirty car. Write this in the circle marked number 2.

3. **Determine the halfway point from where you are now and where you want to be.**

   Step 3 describes the halfway point. You have cleaned the outside of the car, but the inside is still filthy. Write the halfway point in number 3 circle.

4. **Determine the mid-point between that halfway point and the goal.**

   Step 4 is halfway between Step 3 and Step 1 (the mid-point between that halfway point and the goal). You have cleared the rubbish out of the car and are just about to start cleaning the inside of the car.

5. **Figure out your first step.**

   Step 5 (which is your first step) is getting your bucket ready, the cleaning solution out, and putting on your wellies ready to start cleaning the outside of your car.

Here is a real life example of how to achieve your goal for your 5-year business plan.

1. **You've defined that you want to achieve a £1,000,000 turnover in a year.**

   Write this goal in the number 1 circle.

2. **Describe where you are now – the turnover is currently £250,000 and you have *x* number of clients.**

   Put this information in circle number 2.

3. **Write down the halfway point in number 3 circle.**

   That is when your turnover is £500,000 and you have increased your client base.

4. **You have continued to increase your client base and your turnover.**

   Write down the halfway point between Step 3 and Step 1 (the mid-point between that halfway point and your goal).

5. **Decide how to increase your client base by getting together a team of people to discuss new advertising and sales options.**

   Place the option with the most support in circle number 5.

   It's now apparent that your first step when faced with the daunting task of increasing your turnover to £1,000,000 is to carry out the option described in circle 5.

Prioritising Your Goals

Sorting out your priorities can help you decide how important a goal is for you. You can use a scoring system, described in the next section, to prioritise your goal.

 Think about the difference between a task that is urgent and a task that is important. An urgent task is not necessarily important to *you*, but may be urgent because of a timescale created by someone else. For example, many managers dread the monthly report they are obliged to write and delay starting it. It's not important to them, but the report becomes urgent as the deadline set by the organisation approaches.

Deciding the focus

Deciding which key areas to focus on is important, and you should include both short-term and long-term priorities. The following list shows ten key areas:

- ✔ Family and home life
- ✔ Work and career
- ✔ Relationships and friends
- ✔ Health and fitness, including personal appearance
- ✔ Travel and recreation, including holidays
- ✔ Financial security, including investments, pensions, money for school fees
- ✔ Personal and/or spiritual development, including hobbies and pastimes
- ✔ Improving confidence and self-esteem
- ✔ Community work
- ✔ Personal possessions

Figure 5-2 provides a visual representation to help clarify your key goals.

1. **Start by writing each of these ten areas into a segment of the wheel.**

2. **Assign a number to each segment of the wheel based on how important it is to you to achieve your goal.** As you place numbers in each section of the wheel you start to prioritise your goals. The goals with the highest numbers are your priorities.

3. **Choose your top three areas to focus on.**

If financial security is your top goal, you can break this down further in the following ways:

✔ Finding a more secure job

✔ Asking for a salary increase

✔ Achieving your sales target and end of year bonus

✔ Moving house to reduce your mortgage

✔ Putting money into a pension plan

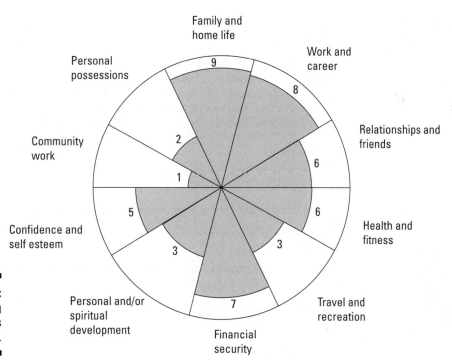

Figure 5-2:
Creating
your focus
wheel.

Goals taking you into retirement

Leela has had several goals since retiring. Using the wheel shown in Figure 5-2 helped her prioritise her top three goals and take steps to achieving them. Her goals are to maintain her fitness, become involved in community work, and continue her hobby of painting.

After prioritising her goals Leela worked out what she needed to do to keep herself focused:

✔ **Fitness:** To maintain her fitness she arranged to go for a walk every Wednesday with three friends. She wrote this into her diary as a weekly commitment. She also decided to walk to the local shop to buy her paper every day, which would take her about 20 minutes.

✔ **Community work:** To become involved in some community work Leela approached the local nursing home to see if volunteer drivers or visitors were needed. She also contacted the local Citizens' Advice Bureau to find out what other opportunities were available for volunteer work in the local area.

✔ **Hobbies:** To continue her hobby of painting Leela enrolled at the local college for weekly art classes.

Choosing quick wins

Quick wins are those tasks that you know you can complete quickly and easily and that contribute to achieving your goal. Quick wins provide instant results to keep you motivated, and help you feel that you're making progress towards your key goals. A quick win can improve your confidence and belief that you can really achieve your goal and helps you to feel good about yourself.

For example, a quick win is something you can achieve at once, this week or this month, rather than in five years' or ten years' time. The following list includes a few examples:

✔ Deciding to complete the easiest section of your monthly report first

✔ Tidying the smallest drawer of the filing cabinet rather than tackling the whole office

✔ Edging the lawn instead of mowing the lot improves the look of your garden

✔ Just vacuuming the carpet if you don't have time to clean the whole house before your guests arrive

✔ Putting dates in your diary for team meetings, before tackling all the meeting preparations

Dividing goals into achievable chunks

After you've prioritised your goals, breaking them down into bite-sized chunks makes them easier to achieve and helps you to maintain your motivation. Looking at a task as a series of manageable steps, rather than just looking at the end goal, helps you stop feeling overwhelmed. The uphill struggle fades into the distance.

If your goal is to move house, some of the smaller achievable steps can include

- Contacting estate agents to register your interest and define your requirements
- Obtaining details of potential properties to view
- Searching the Internet
- Driving around several areas to view possible locations
- Reviewing your budget and mortgage

Peter wanted to feel less out of breath when playing football with his son. To make his goal achievable, he broke it into smaller chunks. The first chunk was to contact his friend Joe. The second chunk was to commit time in his diary to walk with Joe for an hour each week for four weeks. It was only a weekly commitment, and a small step, to help towards his goal of improving his fitness, but it provided Peter with the motivation to get himself started.

Facing Your Demons

Your *demons* are aspects of your life that hold you back from making changes or doing something different. Even though you are motivated, your demons can stop you achieving your goals!

Taking one bite at a time!

Remember the old saying – How do you eat an elephant? Answer 'one bite at a time'!

When I am writing, my quick wins are the completion of smaller sections within each chapter, so that I can see the book taking shape. I initially map out the key areas and tackle some of the smaller sections first so I feel I am making progress.

'Demons' are sometimes just statements or excuses. How often have you heard people say the following?

- When I have time, I will do . . .
- One day I will get round to . . .
- Later I will tackle . . .
- I'll start next week
- I just can't get going
- I'll just do this first
- Other things are more important at the moment
- I'm not sure where to start
- It feels too complicated to me
- The benefits do not seem to be worth the effort
- I'm scared to tackle it
- I've never done it before
- It's not worth trying because I know I'll fail
- I can't face starting this because my mother always told me I would be useless at it
- When I was 8 years old my teacher laughed at me when I spoke in class and now I can't do public presentations

What other personal favourites do you use that hinder you from achieving your goals?

In other contexts, 'demons' can be those tasks which suddenly *must* be done before you can tackle anything contributing to achieving your goal. The demon can be a goal in itself.

Identifying your demons

Your demons can include the following:

- Household chores or maintenance jobs that you keep putting off
- An attic that is never cleared
- Papers that are left piling up
- Filing that never gets done

✔ Phone calls not returned

✔ Utility bills that are not paid

✔ Friends you don't get round to contacting

✔ A project that you haven't managed to start

✔ A report that's not written

✔ A tax return still waiting to be done

Note down any of the preceding demons that apply to you! You can also write your own list of personal demons. Coming face to face with the demons helps you see what is stopping you from tackling your goal.

Build in tackling your demons as part of your steps toward achieving your goal. Try to identify what, in particular, is holding you back from starting to work on your goal. For example, if you tidied your desk, did your filing, or cleaned your home office, would you feel more motivated to tackle your goal?

Tackling your demons to keep you motivated towards your goals

After being honest with yourself and identifying your demons, you're ready to tackle them. How you tackle your demons differs from person to person. Often, the very act of acknowledging and facing your demons is enough to make them go away.

The influence of your mother-in-law

A friend was feeling very demotivated after the Christmas holidays. She needed to develop her home business further to generate new clients, but was finding it hard to get going and make any decisions about new advertising and promotion.

What eventually spurred her into action was a call from her mother-in-law arranging to come and stay! My friend immediately vacuumed the whole house, tidied up the children's rooms, and cleaned the kitchen. The big clear-up made her feel more energised and more positive to start working on her important goal of developing the business. The untidy house had been like a 'demon' causing her period of stagnation. Once she had dealt with the demon and cleaned the house, she felt motivated to plan a strategy to gain new clients to grow her business.

On a personal note, I was told at school that I wasn't good at geography. To this day, I have to tackle this demon by saying 'I am good at geography'. This is enough to have the effect of making me confident with map reading and, in most situations, not getting lost.

Sometimes, imagining shutting them in the cupboard can help! You could also try writing your demons down as an action list or talking to a colleague to help you spur yourself into action. You could commit time in your diary to deal with them, or face your demons up front so that you have to deal with them right now! For example, if your demon is tackling a technology issue with your computer, it is better to give it a go and risk making a mistake rather than continuing to do nothing. You often learn something new from the experience, which helps you face the demon.

The phrase 'just do it' is very appropriate. A call from your mother-in-law about an impending visit may catapult you into action! Take a look around you. Is there anything that you can see which may be stopping you working on your goals? Are there some tasks you really have to do first? Some important errands to do, phone calls to make, meetings to attend? Do them today, praise yourself, and enjoy the good feeling. Having put the demons behind you, you are now in the right frame of mind to focus on your goals.

Chapter 6

Maintaining Motivation
Now and Beyond

. . . .

In This Chapter

▶ Envisioning motivation in your life

▶ Recognising what gets you moving

. . . .

*W*ell done! You've summoned up the motivation to get going on that all-important project. You're off to a great start. However, staying motivated is key to the success of achieving your goal. In this chapter, I suggest a variety of techniques to keep yourself motivated, especially when you find yourself wavering after the initial excitement of performing your task loses its momentum.

Visualising Motivation

Visualisation means imagining a particular situation in your mind – such as what it will actually be like living in the new house you're saving up for, or meeting up with your old classmates at the school reunion; none of you having changed a bit! Visualisation is a powerful way of getting your mental muscles working to picture goals or aspirations in your mind's eye before the event actually occurs. The mind doesn't know the difference between what is imagined and what is actual. Take the example of visualising a perfect golf or tennis shot. You imagine it in your mind as if it was really happening in a perfect way, even though you haven't yet hit the ball. This acts as a dress rehearsal so that when you do actually hit the ball you've already 'rehearsed' the shot in your mind.

So when you get moving on the task that you've visualised, your brain thinks it has already performed the action.

Visualisation can work for you in any situation, at home and at work. Sight is, of course, the main sense used in visualisation: But using your other senses of smell, hearing, touch, and taste makes the technique even more powerful.

Here's a snapshot of how the visualisation technique works:

1. **Take a moment to think back to your last holiday.**

   Close your eyes to blot out any distractions going on around you.

2. **Recall as many details of your holiday as you can.**

   Where did you stay; who were you with; what were you doing; what were you wearing; what was the weather like; what were people talking about; how did you feel? As you bring the images of your holiday into your mind, make the images as colourful as you can by using all your senses to heighten the experience.

3. **As you recall the holiday, imagine opening your eyes: see what is around you, listen to the sounds, and concentrate on what you are feeling.**

   You may also want to bring into play your other senses of taste, touch, and smell.

You have just been on a journey into your mind. Having rehearsed the technique of visualisation you can now plan future events, visualising what you want the outcome to be.

The more detail you bring into your visualisation, the better your result.

Seeing your success

Your visual sense allows you to bring images into your mind, as if you are painting a picture. Use a full palette of colours, experimenting with light and dark, sun and shade. Try adding movement to your picture, making it run like a movie.

Practise changing your picture from black and white to full colour, and a still image to a moving picture. Seeing yourself playing a central role as if you're the lead actor or actress helps to make your visualisation stronger and more powerful.

Gauging your feelings

As you visualise completing a task or achieving a goal, be aware of what feelings you're experiencing and how they're affecting your body. Practise increasing the intensity of your feelings as if you were turning up the light on a dimmer switch or flicking a dial from 0 to 10, with '0' recording 'not feeling anything' to '10' being 'intense'.

To highlight your feelings, think back to past situations where you experienced intense feelings or emotions, both good and bad. For example, how you felt when you passed an important exam, or what it was like for you when you were unsuccessful in getting a promotion. Ask yourself how you're going to deal with the positive or negative feelings of the situation. Whereabouts in your body are your feelings strongest? If you want to increase the intensity of the positive feeling, what do you need to do or think about?

Take the example of winning an award. The more you remind yourself of the day you received the award, how you felt, what people were saying to you, the smile on your face, and your sense of elation, the more you secure the memory in your body. As you continue to remind yourself of that day you are reinforcing and strengthening the memory further, so you can call upon the experience again in the future.

Hearing the praise

Hearing your own voice and the voices of other people in your visualisation intensifies your feeling of actually being present. To bring your image to life further, try experimenting with different tones of voice, accents, tempo, loudness and quiet, as if adjusting the volume on a radio or sound system.

Imagining hearing words of praise from friends, family, work colleagues, or an audience giving you a round of applause helps you to maintain your motivation. Remember, as well as hearing, your visualisation can also include silence and a feeling of peace.

Visualise having set yourself the task of clearing out your spare room. You're motivated by the end result of having a tidy room that you can use and being able to find things again! You visualise hearing your partner's praise and feeling proud at a job well done. Running this image several times through your mind cements its power and keeps you motivated.

Using visualisation to rehearse a task or to imagine reaching a goal can strengthen your motivation to continue with a real life task. During visualisation your unconscious mind plays the event as if it's happening now as each aspect of your task is imagined. It's like switching on a set of lights, striking up an orchestra, and stirring together a mixture of feelings.

To make your visualisation work for you, be specific about the sounds, colours, and sensations in your image so that it's strong and powerful. Find yourself a quiet place where you won't be disturbed and think about inspirational and motivating quotations and sayings. As you hear the words or phrases, try imagining the situation from a different perspective and visualise yourself achieving the same goals the inspirational presenter is describing. Visualisation techniques have been used successfully with activities such as fire-walking and Outward Bounds. Using the techniques is a powerful tool for imagining what it feels like to be successful and motivated.

Travelling through time

Picture yourself following a woodland path free from obstruction or walking alongside a sparkling, flowing stream. As you pass through a clearing in the trees or come to a bend in the river, notice the milestones: how far you are along the route, what you've seen and heard, the time the journey is taking, how you're feeling. Visualising yourself travelling through time and successfully passing each milestone increases your motivation to achieve your goal.

Visualisation is a powerful technique but you need to practise it regularly to keep it in working order so your desired outcome remains in the forefront of your mind.

Propelling Yourself Forward

Discovering what drives you forward is key to keeping yourself motivated. Think about the motivation behind the following goals:

- ✔ Winning a competition motivates you to get the job finished on time.

- ✔ Taking part and completing a fun run motivates you to exercise regularly.

- ✔ A financial reward motivates you to work harder.

- ✔ Looking good in that expensive new outfit motivates you to eat less and exercise more.

- ✔ Achieving public recognition in your job motivates you to pursue your ambition of a career change.

You can find yourself being propelled into action for both positive and negative reasons – like exercising daily to increase fitness or exercising daily merely to stop yourself getting ill. (Chapter 3 has more on this topic.)

Sophie attends my weekly Pilates classes. She knew she ought to practise Pilates at home in between the weekly classes, but she kept finding reasons not to do so. She had a DVD of Pilates exercises lying unused on the kitchen table. By chance Sophie found the key to propelling herself forward into action. Sophie discovered she just needed to put a specific time aside for Pilates practice by saying to herself 'I'm going to exercise at 10 am' Saying 'I'll exercise *sometime* today' just didn't work. Interestingly, Sophie also said she had to 'get rid of her mother' before she could get on with her exercises. Her mother stays with her often and Sophie realised she felt inhibited if her mother was watching over her!

Watching the *Strictly Come Dancing* series on the BBC you have to admire the amazing bodies of the professional dancers. Their toned muscles show off their dance outfits to perfection. In one series, the professional Italian dancer, Flavia Cacace, caught the eye of the audience by showing her stomach muscle definition in a Latin dancing outfit. One of the newspaper headlines read 'The Six Pack that Seduced a Nation'. I teach Pilates and several clients asked me how they could achieve Flavia's 'Six Pack'! Flavia has been dancing since the age of 6 and is the Argentinian Tango World Champion. Like many professional dancers she trains for five to six hours a day using a combination of exercises to maintain her fitness, dancing ability, and muscle definition. Seeing Flavia performing on TV was an inspiration to many people who were propelled forward into joining dance classes.

Once I was coaching an 18-year-old boy in revision techniques for his forthcoming exams. He had trouble settling down to revision; he simply couldn't see the point of it. He felt pressured by his parents, who he said 'nagged him constantly' to get on with his revision. What eventually propelled him forward to start revising seriously wasn't the prospect of getting better exam results to help him in his future career, but stopping his parents' ceaseless nagging!

What propels you forward? Do the following strike a chord?

- ✔ The enjoyment of a day's rowing inspires you to get your sculling boat out of storage and take up rowing again.

- ✔ The embarrassment of turning up late for a business appointment and losing the contract causes you to rush out to purchase a satellite navigation system.

- ✔ The fear of doing a bad presentation at a conference propels you into cancelling your weekend away in order to practise and perfect your presentation techniques.

- ✔ The anger or hurt you feel after a disagreement with an old friend forces you to confront the issue rather than avoiding it.

Think about your goals for this coming week and month. Then decide what factors are likely to propel you forward and keep you motivated to achieve your goals. The following sections suggest ways of helping you to propel yourself toward your goals.

Acknowledging your success

Experiencing a 'feel good' factor when you've completed a job often serves to encourage you to tackle the next task, minor or major. Taking time to acknowledge your success is a great way of motivating yourself to achieve future goals.

Do any of the following give you a glow of satisfaction at a job well done?

- ✔ Paying the bills

- ✔ Phoning an elderly relative

- ✔ Replying to your backlog of emails

- ✔ Reading and digesting a business report

- ✔ Doing the monthly food shopping

- ✔ Clearing your wardrobe

- ✔ Putting together a business proposal

- ✔ Finishing your VAT or accounts

- ✔ Sweeping up the piles of autumn leaves

- ✔ Completing a performance appraisal with a difficult member of staff

- ✔ Concluding a difficult negotiation

- ✔ Finishing a project on time and on budget

Acknowledge your achievement by saying 'well done', treating yourself to a reward, or just taking time to feel pleased with yourself. Choosing to personally acknowledge your own success or preferring to hear yourself praised by other people is called being internally or externally referenced:

- ✔ **Internally referenced** people get a positive feeling when they know they have done a good job. They feel happy inside themselves and don't usually need to hear praise from other people.

  For example, a colleague prefers to write under a pseudonym – she is internally referenced, not needing to receive praise from others. She describes how she 'gets her glow' just by enjoying the writing, rather

> than having her work being published under her real name and being given public recognition.
>
> ✔ **Externally referenced** people like to have their success publicly acknowledged. For example, by hearing positive comments from colleagues, and seeing published reports of their achievements.

Sometimes in personal relationships you find that partners have quite opposite views on acknowledging success. One partner may demand praise while the other is content to do without. Likewise in business, individual members of a team may need to be praised in order to feel motivated to contribute to the team effort, while other team members are happy to do without praise, happy in the knowledge they are doing a good job.

Performance appraisals are valuable for acknowledging and praising staff for their achievements. A successful performance appraisal can motivate and spur an employee to achieve both personal and company goals.

Decide whether you are internally or externally referenced and use praise and success to drive your motivation accordingly.

I run training courses and I find feedback from the participants invaluable – usually gathered from evaluation forms. I value the comments as they are important for motivating myself to run the courses. Recently I made a presentation at a European conference, but giving out evaluation forms wasn't possible for logistical reasons. After the presentation I received a spontaneous round of applause, and the comments from individual delegates afterwards gave me the external praise I much needed and which is so important to my motivation.

Steering a clear course

To keep yourself and the team motivated and on course, revise your action plan from time to time to build in any necessary changes. Being flexible, trying alternatives, perhaps bringing in new people, and changing a timescale help to keep you and the team motivated.

For example, an experienced yachtsman knows which way she's heading. She charts a clear course, using the right sails according to the direction of the wind, its strength, and tides. The skilled yachtsman constantly makes adjustments to her course, taking into account weather conditions, yacht performance, competence of the crew, and confidence in the boat, and herself.

Clearing the garage!

Jan and Gary were well known for the terrible state of their garage. It had become such a dumping ground that they could no longer shut the door properly and they hadn't used it for many a year for its original purpose – to park the car. Jan and Gary were always saying 'we must tidy the garage', but it never happened.

Being interested in what motivates people led me to ask them why they never got around to clearing and tidying out the garage. What I discovered was fascinating. It transpired that 'a tidy garage' was not the goal for either of them. (Neither of them rate tidiness very highly.) For Gary, the garage was somewhere to hang up his numerous DIY tools so that he could see what he had and find them when he needed them. For Jan, the garage was somewhere to keep her car warm and dry so that in the winter she didn't have to stand outside in the freezing cold scraping the ice off her windscreen. Armed with this information, I was able to get Jan and Gary to each visualise what a clear and tidy garage would look like. Gary visualised

having space to hang his tools; Jan imagined having somewhere to shelter her car from the bad weather.

Using the visualisation techniques described in this chapter, Gary saw, in his mind's eye, his tools hanging neatly on the wall. I got him to increase the colour of his picture, and he said that his tools were all bright and shiny. He could hear himself saying 'I'll just go and get my drill' and he felt the pleasure at being able to put his hands on the right tools for the job. Jan visualised having the space to easily park her car in the garage. Jan extended her visualisation to a wintry morning and felt the pleasure of being free of having to scrape the frost off her windscreen.

Cleaning the garage took several weekends to finish but, by rerunning their separate visualisations, Jan and Gary kept their motivation going to complete the task. Although they were motivated for entirely different reasons, they were both able to propel themselves forward to achieve a common goal.

Maintaining your motivation involves steering a clear course and responding to the daily challenges. Your goal may stay the same, but you may find that your course needs to be corrected. Decide how you need to adjust to daily challenges to keep yourself motivated.

Many years ago I worked in Australia for the Royal Flying Doctor Service. We flew in an ancient twin-engine plane quite different from the modern ones used today. Our pilot was in the habit of describing clearly and in detail his flight plan as we flew over the remote Australian outback to pick up a patient. The pilot constantly checked his progress, anticipating events that may affect our course and was always prepared for emergencies. There were many occasions when he had to change his flight path because of weather conditions or because he had to pick up another injured person.

I saw a fascinating programme on TV about Raymond Blanc's Michelin starred restaurant, Le Manoir de Quatre Saisons. The programme showed the wonderful Oxfordshire house and gardens where his restaurant is located, portraying the restaurant as a centre of excellence. Viewing the vegetable gardens, the freshly home-grown produce, and the pictures of the dedicated chefs preparing exquisite dishes inspired me to treat myself to a meal at this world famous restaurant.

Chapter 7

Dealing with Setbacks

*T*oo often people view setbacks in a negative light. In this chapter, you look at the positive side of setbacks – how they can give you the opportunity to change direction or start afresh. I also show you how to overcome obstacles and keep yourself motivated and the value of having contingency plans in place to keep you on track.

Overcoming Setbacks and Struggles

Acknowledging that you're struggling to keep motivated is your first positive step toward overcoming a setback. You may think you face an impossible task – the very word 'struggle' conjures up pictures in your mind of strife, upheaval, pressure, challenges, delays, conflict, and more!

Often your finest achievements are the ones where you struggled greatest. Maintaining motivation is often challenging, and you can find yourself struggling, but if the task is too easy it won't keep you sufficiently motivated.

A course I run includes techniques for speed reading – a method of very rapid reading to help manage the huge volume of documents, papers, and reports, which many people have to deal with every day. Speed reading techniques involve training the eye muscles to work in a different way. Speed reading is a skill: it takes time, effort, and practice to achieve results. If it was easy everyone would be able to speed read naturally. In a similar way, keeping motivated and overcoming setbacks takes effort and practice. And you may need to discover new techniques along the way to keep you going.

Understanding setbacks

You have carefully planned your course of action and made difficult decisions – then an obstacle rears its ugly head when you least expect it. It can be very frustrating to find that things aren't going according to plan. Setbacks can occur for countless reasons: timescales are altered, changes in personnel, resources, weather, illness, family or work commitments, accidents, customer or client demand. Events appear to have conspired against you; preventing you moving forward or completing your task.

However, setbacks are a normal part of everyday life. Can you think of an example where a setback caused you to change course, with the result that your new approach is proving to be more fruitful and positive? Or, you may know of someone who wasn't successful with a job interview, only to find the next job he applied for turned out to match his particular skills so much better. And anyone involved in buying a house knows only too well there are going to be setbacks – far too many!

You could experience a minor setback (such as a contractual delay when buying a house, delaying the completion date) or alternatively, a major setback (such as not being able to purchase your chosen house) sending you right back to square one again. How you assess the situation and your actions will depend on whether the delay is a minor setback or a major hurdle. If the latter is the case you may need to reassess if you're on the right path or change tack completely. Dealing with a minor delay just involves gearing yourself up again.

A setback often contains a valuable hidden message. You need to be ready to listen to what the message is telling you. Sometimes you may have to look more deeply to find the hidden message. Be honest with yourself. Ask 'what is causing the slip back?' Make a fresh start (refer to Chapter 3), and keep asking yourself 'what is stopping me?' and refocusing on the end goal. Take any feedback on board and use it in your future plans.

Psychologists and motivational experts often refer to the quotation 'There is no such thing as failure, only feedback'. This invites you to think of what others might see as failure as an opportunity to receive feedback.

Success comes from keeping on trying. Take the example of Joe, who failed his driving test several times. Each time he failed he became very despondent and nearly gave up his driving lessons. His instructor took the time to explain the areas he needed to improve. The feedback was valuable for Joe. Each driving test failure turned into an extra lesson, making Joe an even better driver when he eventually passed his test.

If at first you don't succeed, try, try, and try again!

Years ago I was working for a large healthcare company that was undergoing major reorganisation. The medical team, of which I was part, was being restructured and many people in the team, including myself, faced redundancy. We were all consulted during the restructuring process but it was a difficult time for everyone. The whole process was extremely unsettling as we all tried to decide whether to apply for other jobs in the same organisation or look for another job elsewhere.

Looking back I realise what a great opportunity being made redundant turned out to be. I set up my own health consultancy company. This turned out to be a very positive move, although at the time I thought that redundancy was a major setback, but it proved to be the springboard for further training, networking with new people, and gaining independence. New avenues of opportunity opened up for me which wouldn't have happened if I had stayed working for my old company.

Seeing the positive

Next time you experience a setback at work or at home, ask yourself the following questions:

- ✔ What's the reason for the setback?
- ✔ What can I do instead?
- ✔ Is there a different approach I can take?
- ✔ What other people can I now involve?
- ✔ What does this free me up to do?
- ✔ Can I take a different perspective?
- ✔ Are there going to be any financial advantages?
- ✔ Is my alternative plan going to be more effective?
- ✔ Do I need to be more flexible?
- ✔ How can I tackle things differently?

Be flexible and look for the positive outcome created by the setback and focus on new options that perhaps didn't occur to you first time round.

A setback can be a voyage of discovery. An invaluable opportunity to try something new. If you feel you are still struggling, you may need to approach the setback in a different way – asking yourself what you can do, instead of focusing on what you can't do.

Reminding yourself of the benefits

If you find yourself struggling to overcome a setback, try constantly reminding yourself of the bigger picture. For example, when I am writing I hold a picture of the completed book in my mind so I don't allow myself to become demotivated if I don't get to the stage I hoped for.

Recently, I was working with a group of MBA students helping them prepare for a series of networking events with major businesses, giving the students the opportunity to find a new job or career advancement. A few of the students weren't looking forward to the events because they didn't like the thought of walking into a room full of people they didn't know. To help the students overcome their dread of the events, I encouraged them to remind themselves of the benefits they would gain from attending. They came to realise how important the business events were for meeting a future employer and for their careers. Throwing themselves in the deep end and having the courage to introduce themselves to new people made it easier for them in the long run to make new contacts and secure future clients.

Thinking about the overall benefits of changing direction or taking on a new project is important. The benefits are likely to be different for each project you tackle as well as for each individual. Here are a number of benefits from overcoming a setback and starting again:

- ✔ Gaining promotion
- ✔ Greater financial rewards
- ✔ Meeting new people
- ✔ Acquiring new skills
- ✔ Rising to a challenge
- ✔ Reaching your goal
- ✔ Winning a new contract
- ✔ Moving out of a difficult relationship
- ✔ Travelling to foreign parts
- ✔ Improving communication skills

Taking time out to review how your project is progressing can help you and your team see the benefits that your hard work is bringing, and helps to maintain motivation and keep everyone on track.

Refocusing on the rewards

Rewards act as an incentive for keeping yourself motivated to finish a task. (For more about rewards go to Chapter 8.) Keeping your mind fixed on the benefits you're likely to gain from overcoming a setback can sharpen your focus and lessen your struggle.

Early on in my career I won a travel prize to the United States to work on a project involving wellness at work. The application and interview processes were extremely gruelling, but I was determined to win, having a clear picture of the benefits I would gain from the trip. The reward was worth all the effort, and the experience of working in the US opened up for me many new career opportunities.

'When the going gets tough the tough get going'. Keep yourself on track by reminding yourself that each hurdle is there to help you become stronger and more focused.

Creating Contingency Plans

Setbacks can throw you off balance, but having a back-up plan in place in case the unexpected happens helps you stay on course and keeps you motivated to achieve your goal.

Contingency plans can range from a simple plan B to an official crisis strategy document used by a company or hospital. A contingency plan helps you cope with the unexpected event in a calm and stress-free manner, making sure you're able to deal with the task in hand.

Have you needed to make use of any of the following contingency plans over the last few months?

- ✔ **Building costs:** Building in a 10 per cent margin in anticipation of the rise in the price of building materials for a new extension

- ✔ **Travel and transport:** Getting an up-to-date list of taxi services and hotels in case you miss a flight, train connection, or last bus home

- ✔ **Meeting up:** Fixing a landmark as a meeting place should members of the group get separated or lost

- ✔ **Contact numbers:** Having a list of phone numbers in the car in the event of getting held up on the motorway or involved in an accident

- ✔ **Staff cover:** Arranging an open-ended contract with your stand-in at work in case your recovery from illness takes longer than expected

- ✔ **Duplicate documents:** Copying passport and important travel documents should the originals be lost or stolen

- ✔ **Freezer well-stocked:** Making sure extra foodstuffs are at hand for feeding unexpected visitors

- ✔ **Plumbing:** Creating a handy list of phone numbers of local plumbers for emergencies, together with the location of the stopcock

- ✔ **Computer back-up:** Having contact details of employees in hard copy in case of system or power failure

Knowing who to call on for help

When you find yourself having to deal with an unexpected event, having back-up in place and knowing who to call on can be vital. Your support system can include friends, family, neighbours, colleagues, and professionals.

ANECDOTE

Contingency plans in action

A couple of summers ago I was inspired to have a garden party because the weather was hot, sunny, and reliable – or so I thought. The garden was looking its best, tables and chairs were set out, caterers organised, and guests invited. I had two small gazebos for the caterers *just in case* it rained, but knew there was no way I could fit the 50 or so guests inside as well. My plan was, if the heavens opened, to move everyone indoors. On the morning of the garden party thunder rolled and the rain came down in torrents. I moved the gazebos nearer to the house but unfortunately the rain poured off them and flooded the entrance. At this stage what you needed most was a pair of Wellington boots! Added to this, all the approach roads were flooded, delaying all the guests.

When the guests eventually arrived we all gathered indoors only to find that, within half an hour, magically the weather changed, the rain stopped, and the sun shone brilliantly. Without hesitation my guests rushed outdoors, the party got off the ground and proved to be a great success. I found out a lot about dealing with setbacks that day. All the guests remarked on how well I had managed the day, moving guests from outdoors to indoors and back again, and said it was a garden party they wouldn't forget. What I initially thought was a setback, that the weather was going to ruin my party, turned out to be the exact opposite. The atrocious weather had made it a day to remember!

Have you experienced any of the following?

> ✔ Calling on family and friends to collect your child from school when you get delayed
>
> ✔ Leaving an emergency key with neighbours
>
> ✔ Keeping a list of emergency telephone numbers by the phone
>
> ✔ Setting up care lines or call buttons for an elderly person living alone
>
> ✔ Having weekend contact numbers of colleagues for a business emergency
>
> ✔ Programming ICE numbers into your mobile phone

Key the word ICE into your list of contacts on your mobile phone. It stands for *in case of emergency*. Under this entry, list the telephone numbers of those people to be contacted on your behalf in case of an emergency. All emergency services personnel are trained to search a person's mobile phone for an ICE entry.

Updating your action plan

Make sure your action plan is up to date. If something unforeseen happens you may need, for example, to amend your timescales, bring in different people, or adjust your budgets.

Timescales are particularly important to some people. Set down the times-cales in your action plan *as it is today*. Action plans should always be updated when new information comes to light. However, don't put off writing your action plan just because you don't have every single detail at hand.

Knowing When Fear Affects You

Fear is a very strong emotion, especially when you face a dangerous situation. Likewise, fear can affect your motivation and stop you carrying out necessary tasks. You can experience fear in a variety of ways and with different degrees of severity depending on how you react to the situation. One person may experience a real sense of danger in a particular situation while another person finds the same situation merely a challenge.

Fear can potentially cause a setback, stopping you moving forward because you're scared of what might happen. Fear can paralyse any action until you face and overcome it.

Take the example of grieving after a loved one dies. Many people need to face the first anniversary of the death before they feel they are able to move forward. As they approach the anniversary, the fear of being overwhelmed with grief causes a setback to the grieving process.

The brain transmits your feelings of fear to your body. Adrenaline is released quickly into your body, preparing you for flight or fight. As the hormone adrenaline is released, there's a surge of energy within the body. If this energy isn't used up, panic occurs. A feeling of pressure can build up inside the body, like a pressure cooker, quite often affecting how you react to other people, like suddenly shouting at a friend or colleague or displaying road rage. The pressure can also cause feelings of anxiety, despair, and depression.

Figure 7-1 shows the variety of symptoms that can occur when you experience fear or hostility. The symptoms are caused by adrenaline travelling around your body.

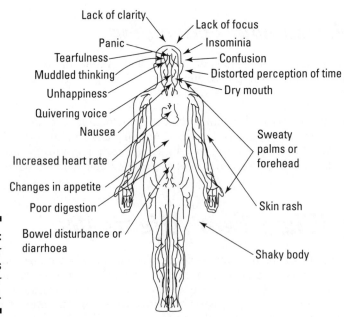

Figure 7-1: How your body reacts to fear or hostility.

Labels (left side): Lack of clarity, Panic, Tearfulness, Muddled thinking, Unhappiness, Quivering voice, Nausea, Increased heart rate, Changes in appetite, Poor digestion, Bowel disturbance or diarrhoea

Labels (right side): Lack of focus, Insominia, Confusion, Distorted perception of time, Dry mouth, Sweaty palms or forehead, Skin rash, Shaky body

If you experience any of these symptoms, and they aren't connected to fear, you must contact your doctor for advice.

When you feel fear, remind yourself the unpleasant symptoms are caused by the hormones in your body, not the situation itself. The action of accepting the feeling of fear is your first step to getting rid of the symptoms.

Once I was in the situation of trying to help a couple get over their fear of moving house. Their house sold very quickly, and they were faced with moving into a rented house while looking for a property to buy. Unexpectedly, they experienced a fear of letting go of their familiar surroundings and friends and neighbours. They described their fear as if it was like 'jumping without a parachute'. They didn't like the idea of moving into a temporary home that wasn't their own. The couple had created an imaginary brick wall of fear in their minds. I spent time coaching them to look over the wall and see the rented house as a stepping stone to their future. Talking through their situation gave them both the momentum and motivation to confront their fear of leaving the familiar and embracing the new. Soon after my coaching sessions, the couple moved into their rented house. When I went to see them, they were busy putting up pictures and making their rented house feel like a home. They overcame their fear of unfamiliar surroundings and were now able to move forward. I was delighted to hear that in their words 'they were 80 per cent there!'

Facing the fear

When you face a difficult situation, you can find yourself struggling to think clearly, and it's hard to summon the motivation to confront the fear. You can feel confused and out of control. Letting go of something, or taking the next step forward can also cause fear, as can coping with changes and moving into unknown territory. If you continue to live with your fear rather than confronting it, your fear can get bigger in your mind, stopping you from dealing with it.

Your first step is to admit to feeling the fear. This step is often the hardest. After you acknowledge that feeling of fear, you're halfway to overcoming your fear.

A colleague going through a divorce described the fear she felt about whether she was making the right decision. In her mind, she wanted the divorce but she was frightened of leaving the security of her old home and moving to a completely new area. A divorce also meant facing financial challenges. She was scared about making decisions, so she kept putting the divorce off. She didn't even have the courage to contact her husband. He eventually took the first step and filed for divorce, bringing it home to her that she really needed to move away from the unhappy marriage. To overcome her fear of starting a new life, I encouraged my colleague to write down all her fears and concerns. The process of writing allowed her to be completely honest with herself and identify the specific fears that were stopping her from moving on.

You can choose to confront your fear by talking about it, writing your thoughts down, and bringing your fear to the forefront of your mind. Doing this prepares you for taking action and moving on.

ANECDOTE

Childhood experiences

Getting through childhood fears and coming out unscathed and on top can stand you in good stead in your adult life. When I was a teenager, I went on an activity holiday to learn canoeing and abseiling. Part of the canoeing experience was turning the canoe upside down so you knew how to get out when you were submerged underwater. Facing up to attempting the technique was really hard. I tried reminding myself that I was in a safe situation with experienced people around me, and that I had to get the technique under my belt for my own safety. I went through the technique step by step in my mind. Finally I took the plunge, managing the technique successfully the first time around. By the end of the holiday, I was happily going through the technique without any trouble, though I have to admit sometimes unintentionally! That teenage challenge gave me new-found confidence in myself, and as I grew older I found I was strong enough to face many more challenges.

Another experience I had was while chatting to a lady in her 80s. She told me that when she was about 5 years old her parents went to the local cinema on a Friday evening. Her grandparents stayed in the house, but the 5-year-old child stayed awake in bed all evening, not allowing herself to go to sleep until she heard her parents come safely back home. She never told her parents or her grandparents that she kept herself awake. It was her fear of her parents not coming home that made her act as she did, and no one in the world ever knew.

I wonder how many other children, big or little, are still holding onto fears that they could very well let go?

Ask yourself the following questions if you find yourself facing a difficult or fearful situation:

- ✔ What's stopping me?
- ✔ What thoughts are going through my mind?
- ✔ Is the danger real or imagined?
- ✔ Can the situation be avoided?
- ✔ Who can help me?
- ✔ Is my inaction making the situation worse?
- ✔ What am I scared of doing?
- ✔ What's the worst thing that could happen?
- ✔ Why don't I want to make a change?
- ✔ What do I fear most?

Controlling your fears

Try out the following techniques to help you control and overcome your fear:

- ✔ **Practise.** Face your fear to discover how to overcome it. This means taking action. Sitting at home reading about how to learn to drive is okay, but eventually you have to sit behind the steering wheel and turn the key in the ignition.

- ✔ **Just do it.** Putting things off gets you nowhere and the situation stays the same. Book a slot in your diary to do now whatever you have been putting off.

- ✔ **Take the first step.** After you've made the decision to take the first step to overcome your fear, you're well on your way to change. The next step then becomes easier and propels you forward.

- ✔ **Confront the fear.** If you continue to live with fear you can feel imprisoned and experience more pain. Fear can stop you achieving your goals.

- ✔ **Think of the worst-case scenario.** What's the worst thing that can happen to you? Then tell yourself you will be able to deal with it.

- ✔ **Take courage.** Don't spend your life 'wishing you had done something different', but never had the courage to try.

- ✔ **Look for possible alternatives.** Sometimes you don't need to confront the fear head on, but you can explore other options first.

- ✔ **Take small steps.** You don't need to make major changes straight away. Sometimes taking very small steps is easier; for example, a diver masters the smaller dives first, before attempting to dive off the top board. Taking smaller steps, one at a time, builds up your confidence.

- ✔ **Ask friends for help.** If possible, find a friend who has been in a similar situation.

Part III
Arming Yourself with Motivational Tools

'Ok, so what _else_ has motivated you to want to be a fireman, Mr Trimblott?'

In this part. . .

You have all the tools at your fingertips, you just need to know how and when to use them. In this part, you discover what's going on in your brain and how using your brain can help your motivation. You uncover the secrets of incentives and rewards and the part they play in your overall plan for reaching your goal.

Chapter 8

Using Incentives to Motivate

In This Chapter

▶ Understanding incentives

▶ Choosing incentives

▶ Matching incentives to the situation

Rewards are useful for focusing your mind and your actions, especially when you're having a hard time staying motivated. In this chapter, you explore the importance of incentives and rewards in helping you to reach your goals. I also give you a lot of ideas for rewards that may be appealing to your own special interests.

Benefiting from Incentives at Home and at Work

An *incentive* is a reward that encourages you to make extra effort, such as working harder on a project or creating greater output. The idea behind an incentive is to achieve a goal (refer to Chapter 5). Having a goal influences your actions as you attempt to reach it, and the incentive gives you the motivation to reach your goal.

Incentives can be tangible or intangible. An *intangible incentive* (also called an *intrinsic reward*) has value in making you feel good about yourself. A *tangible incentive* is a financial or material reward giving you public recognition of your achievement. This is also known as an *extrinsic reward*. You can receive both intrinsic and extrinsic rewards; in fact, in many situations, an intrinsic reward is enhanced with an extrinsic reward as well.

Incentives aren't just limited to personal use. In business, incentives are used to motivate and improve performance, recognising and rewarding a job well done. Many companies believe that having an incentive and recognition scheme helps to improve employee performance.

The main benefits for employees of an incentive scheme are the recognition of personal achievement and the feeling of being valued by the employer. Employees often experience higher morale, show company loyalty, and feel empowered when they're rewarded.

Incentives can be made to individuals, a group of employees, or a team working together on a project. The incentive helps to motivate workers to achieve targets.

When ideas are rewarded, people want evidence that their ideas make a difference. The reward then shows management commitment and confidence and encourages people to participate and make quality contributions.

Creating Incentives

Matching the incentive to the individual, group, or organisation is important. If you enjoy chocolate, you'd probably be very pleased to receive a large box of your favourite chocolates! You can experience the same feeling on receiving any unexpected reward.

Whilst writing this chapter, a friend called in unexpectedly and gave me a lovely plant, knowing that I was working hard to finish the book. It was a kind and thoughtful gesture. My friend didn't realise that her gift also encouraged me to keep working – the plant was a very positive incentive for me because I love plants.

At Easter I often give out mini Easter eggs to my Pilates clients after the exercise class. By doing this, I'm rewarding them for their hard work, but also hopefully encouraging them to know they have to keep exercising regularly to maintain their fitness in order to be able to eat the occasional chocolate in the future.

I loved the comment I received from one of my Pilates students. She mentioned how her company offers a variety of cash incentives and prizes to encourage employees to meet certain targets. Most of her colleagues were happy with whatever incentive was on offer but for her it was 'chocolate that worked every time!' You may think chocolates are only a minor incentive. However, if the incentive helps to keep you motivated in achieving your goal, it works.

Different incentives can work in different ways. An incentive driving one person forward can be a huge turn off for another. Check and see how many of the incentives in the following sections match your aspirations.

Personal incentives

Are you having trouble keeping your house spick and span, paying your bills on time, losing weight? Perhaps the following incentives will give you a few ideas.

Health and fitness

Some health insurance companies offer a reduced insurance premium for individuals who can prove they're actively pursuing a healthier lifestyle. For example, health screening; not smoking; losing weight; going to the gym.

Most slimming and weight-management clubs (like Weight Watchers) offer the incentive that, providing you lose weight each week, you don't have to pay your weekly fee.

Gyms offer a special incentive at certain times of the year, waiving the normal membership fee as a way of encouraging new members to join.

Sponsorship

Running the marathon, doing a parachute jump, or taking part in a sponsored walk or sponsored slim are excellent ways of raising cash to support your favourite charity, in the knowledge that you don't want to let your friends down who are sponsoring you.

The MoonWalk women's marathon takes place in England every year. This year, my friend offered an additional massage incentive to her colleague to finish the marathon. The charity benefits financially and her colleague has the feelgood incentive of the massage to look forward to.

Treating yourself to a new outfit

The incentive of buying yourself a new outfit can boost your motivation to finish your home or work project or even to lose those extra few pounds. Not only is it often a great incentive to work hard, but you look forward to wearing the new outfit, which acts as motivation in itself.

Having a weekend away

Having the incentive of visiting a new area, spending a relaxing weekend away, and enjoying some time off encourages you to work hard to win a work contract or finish a house project.

Enjoying a lunch treat

When you have a busy home and working life, having time to enjoy a special lunch or meal out is often a luxury. You could receive the reward for finishing the spring cleaning, helping a friend with a project, or caring for a sick friend.

Rewarding good behaviour

Rewarding good behaviour is very important, especially when children are growing up, and helps them learn the importance of trying hard at school, completing homework, practising their musical instrument, and so on. The reward can be as simple as a 'well done' or a 'thank you', or an incentive offer of a new toy, treat, or day out.

Keeping your children happy

Offering your child or children extra pocket money for keeping their bedroom clean and tidy, or for that special outing, never seems to fail. Having a variety of incentives can be useful, as can finding out what encourages your child to do their best in exams or with a school project.

Training your pet

Training your pet and training yourself go hand in hand. In dog training, rewards are used very effectively to teach dogs to obey, sit and stay, and come to heel. The long-term gain is that both you and your pet are likely to be happier, healthier, and even better company.

Enjoying that cup of coffee

Positive reinforcement (the idea that if we do something right we get a reward or something back) works if it is paired closely with a desired behaviour. You need to be aware of this yourself to set up appropriate rewards and incentives to keep motivated and on track. When you've read this chapter and thought about some of the ideas here, you could reward yourself with a lovely cup of tea or coffee as a positive reinforcement!

The challenge of a speeding fine

Recently a colleague had a speeding fine, after having failed to see the new 30 mile limit sign installed in a previous 40 mile zone. There was no getting out of paying the fine, but she was offered the incentive of not losing any points on her licence, providing she attended a Speed Awareness Course.

Business incentives

If you're a decision-maker in your company, you may want to consider the value provided by offering incentives to your staff. Business incentives can be great at boosting morale, rewarding someone for long hours on a project, or reassuring them that all their extra effort has been noticed. In this way, people often feel more valued and happy to make the extra effort another time.

Many business incentives reward teams, individuals, and employees of the month. Here, I look at some incentive ideas to explore in your own work area.

Team-building adventures

Team-building events are a good way of keeping employees motivated and encouraging employees to work together as a team, as well as giving staff time away from the office in a variety of situations. Team-building helps to improve morale and productivity within the office, with both management and employees benefiting.

Glittering prizes

Salespersons and sales teams are frequently encouraged to reach targets by the use of incentives, often financial. During the time I spent with a large organisation, the sales team was offered a variety of incentives including vouchers for a health farm, hotel vouchers, and theatre tickets. The biggest incentive was the prize to go on a world cruise. Everyone worked incredibly hard throughout the year trying to win the biggest prize.

Pyramid sales companies offer a very clear incentive scheme. Purely based on the amount of sales you achieve, you can reach the bronze, silver, gold, or even platinum level of prizes.

Keeping fit

While working in the occupational health field, I came across enlightened companies providing in-house gym or sports facilities for employees. I was amazed how the offer of a T-shirt, step counter, or sports water bottle was very effective in encouraging employees to take up exercise and attend lunch-time health talks. Even such simple gifts were enough to get employees taking responsibility for their health and welfare.

Flowering around

Do flowers work as an incentive for you? On one occasion I was working on a project with a very tight deadline. I worked very long hours to finish the document, cancelling all my social commitments. After the tender was sub-mitted, we all breathed a sigh of relief. I remember how nice it felt when my manager surprised me by giving me a big bunch of flowers as a thank you. It made me feel good and more committed to help with future projects. My hard efforts were rewarded. However, a well-timed thank you (whether in words or the gift of flowers) can act as a very effective incentive for future commitment.

Rewarding money

For some people, money is the only incentive they will consider! Like the annual bonus for achieving your target, helping you pay for your summer holiday or other necessary expenditure. It is important, though, that the cash reward isn't confused with compensation for overtime or working late.

Financial incentives can come in many other guises. A lot of Internet companies have user-friendly online booking facilities offering cut-price bargains. There are fewer administrative costs for the company and your booking is guaranteed.

Rewarding your team

Anyone who watches *The Apprentice* series on TV knows how, each week, Alan Sugar offers a prize for the winning team. Although staying in the competition and winning is an incentive in itself, the weekly winning team also receives some imaginative rewards, ranging from car rallying, or an expensive meal in a top hotel, to an evening at the opera.

Sports prizes

Winning that coveted trophy, cup, or gold medal is, for many sportsmen and women, an incentive in itself. Realistically however, the addition of a financial prize is an incentive to stay in the game and fund future training.

I remember how happy I felt on school sports day when I won a prize. Several years later when competing in a horse-riding event I was thrilled when I won my first rosette. The simple rosette hung with pride on my bedroom wall for many a year.

Have you won any sports prizes? Did winning act as a powerful incentive to encourage you to train and practise even harder?

Travel vouchers

Travel vouchers are frequently given to customers buying into the company's services. A few years ago my credit card company offered hotel vouchers similar to the Air Miles scheme used by many airlines. I enjoyed a wonderful holiday knowing that my hotel accommodation was being paid for on my 'free' vouchers.

The Air Miles scheme has grown rapidly. It is an effective incentive encouraging you to fly with a particular airline and offering you free flights to destinations around the world.

Using loyalty cards

The revolution in store loyalty cards is fascinating. I know, I have six store cards myself! Each one is for a different product, such as cosmetics and beauty treatments, clothing, household goods, gardening, food, and fuel. I asked around my friends and found that most of us averaged between five and ten loyalty cards each. Every time you use the card you are rewarded with incentive points and special deals. Loyalty cards act as an effective incentive, encouraging you to use a particular store with the promise of rewards points or vouchers in return.

Loyalty cards are obviously a business-promotion strategy for the department stores or restaurants that offer them. However, the reward of money back does seem to motivate people to use a particular store depending on whose offer is best. People are motivated by the feeling that they've got something cheaper or received some money back. The future reward of the loyalty points is the motivating factor to use a particular store.

In business, companies offer clients similar loyalty incentives such as a voucher reward for introducing a friend or the offer of a discount for repeat business.

Cut-price shopping

Alongside loyalty cards is the 'buy one get one free' (sometimes called BOGOF) incentive scheme encouraging shoppers to buy different, and more, products. Even though you didn't really need the extra item, you can be tempted into purchasing the special offer, believing you're getting a good deal.

The cut-price shopping incentives often motivate you to return to that shop, but for some people they can encourage you to buy something you don't really need! So, be aware – are you buying something because it's cheap or because you really need it?

Look at the following cut-price incentives to see if you have been enticed by any of them recently:

- 'Eat all you can' for. . .
- Happy hour (half-price drinks)
- Children eat free
- Special family package
- Two for the price of one
- Free bottle of wine

Exploring Different Incentives for Different Interests

Incentives help people in a variety of ways. However, different interests benefit from different incentives. The size of the incentive needs to match the effort required by the individual, group, or organisation.

Personally speaking: matching your interest to the reward

For one person, the Air Miles scheme is not an incentive, as it's possible to get good deals on the Internet. However, for someone travelling regularly with work, Air Miles is an incentive to use one airline because the rewards can mount up so quickly. Alternatively, the cut-price entry to a theme park won't appeal to a single career woman as much as the family with four children. For the single person, a two-for-one deal at a cinema or restaurant gives them a chance to go with a friend and save money.

For someone in debt, a low-interest credit card is attractive. However, for the person who always pays off their credit card in full each month, the incentive of points or cash is much more appealing.

Choosing the right incentive

Duncan wasn't keen on going for walks. This was unfortunate as his wife, Helena, loved walking and every day she went for a walk along the banks of the nearby Thames. She enjoyed the ever-changing scene on the river, the ducks, and the glorious views across to the Chiltern Hills. Returning home each day she told Duncan about all the interesting things she had seen.

Duncan was slightly more motivated to walk when the weather was sunny, warm, and the grass was dry underfoot. On one such day he went out walking with Helena and was delighted to find that there was a tiny pub hidden away

just past a bend in the river. They stopped for a drink there and Helena was amazed to find that a pint of beer was all the incentive Duncan needed to motivate him to walk regularly. Provided they walked along this route, Duncan willingly went out with her.

Helena's descriptions of the views and wildlife she had seen had left Duncan cold. They were entirely the wrong incentives to get Duncan out walking. Although Helena wasn't much of a drinker she was so delighted at having hit on the right incentive to get Duncan out walking, she was more than happy to go along with him.

Keeping employees happy and motivated: finding the right reward

Many companies have adopted a flexible approach to rewards and benefit schemes, allowing individuals to choose from a variety of incentives. Most of the rewards on offer are given in the form of vouchers rather than a financial bonus.

Here is the menu of the rewards and benefits offered to employees by one company with a large budget:

- **Adventure:** Abseiling, rock climbing, caving
- **Culture:** Concerts, exhibitions, and theatre tickets
- **Driving:** Stock car racing, Ferrari and rallying, tank driving, steam trains
- **Flying:** Gliding, hot-air ballooning, aerobatics, flight simulator
- **Gourmet:** Fine dining, wine-tasting, celebrity cooking
- **Lifestyle:** Boat show, Ideal Home Exhibition, Crufts
- **Pampering:** Health farm, spa days, short breaks
- **Sport:** Archery, golf, horse-riding, dry-slope skiing, snowboarding
- **Water sports:** Sailing, water-skiing, windsurfing, white-water rafting
- **Wildlife and conservation:** Flying an eagle, badger watching, dry-stone walling, big cat weekends

Alternatively, small companies can motivate their staff without spending much money. Some example ideas are:

- A simple employee-of-the-week presentation
- A noticeboard photo of the employee who gave the best customer service that month
- Going home an hour early on Friday if you achieved your weekly sales target
- A personal visit from the managing director to say thank you to the member of staff who demonstrated outstanding behaviour

Always have a variety of incentives on offer, embracing the diversity of people's aspirations. Think carefully about which incentives are going to work best, for the giver and the receiver, and both at home and at work.

Chapter 9

Quizzing Your Brain Cells

. . . . .

In This Chapter

▶ Discovering your motivation ratings

▶ Examining the left and right sides of your brain

▶ Getting yourself mentally fit

. . . . .

*Y*our brain is a powerful computer, having an amazing capacity to store information and record your behaviour. In this chapter, you look into the workings of your brain and how that affects your motivation. You also get the opportunity to check out just how motivated you are and try out some motivational exercises to boost your brain cells.

Scoring Your Personal Motivation

How motivated you are depends on a number of factors; for example, what sort of mood you're in today, what you're working on, the people you're working with. Imagine giving yourself a personal score for how motivated you feel about your task right now. If 'Not motivated' equals a score of '1' and 'Highly motivated' equals a score of '10', what score are you giving yourself?

In Table 9-1 you find a list of questions relating to each motivational area of your task and how committed you are to achieving your task. You can then give yourself a score from 1 to 10 in each motivational area to find out how you're doing.

Table 9-1	My Personal Motivation Score	
Motivational area	*What am I hoping to achieve by completing my task?*	*Score for each motivational area* *1 = Not motivated* *10 = Highly motivated*
Importance	A sense of achievement?	
Reward	Getting a reward – intrinsic or extrinsic – that is going to benefit me? (Refer to Chapter 8 for more on intrinsic and extrinsic rewards.)	
Feel-good factor	Feeling positive and good about myself?	
Benefit to others	Benefits other people?	
Focus	Gives me the opportunity to focus on other areas of my life? (For example, completing the application form is a step towards promotion.)	
Easy to do	Easy to achieve, taking little effort?	
Time-saving	Keeping a record of how I went about the task is going to save time overall and help me to work more efficiently?	
Counting the cost	Avoiding paying a fine or penalty?	

When I asked my colleague Sanjay how motivated he was about completing his VAT return, he said he would give himself a score of 1, but he would give himself a score of 10 for watching television instead! However, realising the benefit of getting his VAT return completed was worth at least 8 on his motivation score, he got on with the task, rewarding himself by watching television later!

In contrast, a friend named TJ scored 10 for being strongly motivated to improve his cooking skills. His wife was going away on holiday with her mother for three weeks and TJ realised that he had just ten days to hone his cooking skills so he wouldn't starve while his wife was away. He sat down with his wife and worked out several menus with her and practised preparing and cooking each meal before she went away.

Raising Your Personal Motivation Score

If you feel the need to improve on your score from Table 9-1 (see the section 'Scoring Your Personal Motivation'), ask yourself the following questions and consider the possible answers:

- Do I need extra resources, for example, adjusting my timescale, more support from other people? *Yes*, moral support from a close colleague is likely to encourage me.

- Do I need to restate my goal? *No.*

- Do I need to break down my task into more manageable chunks? *Yes*, working on one aspect of the task at a time is going to help me to complete my task.

- Is the outcome of my task clear? *Yes.*

- Do I need to apply the SMART goal-setting principles to my task? *Yes*, timescale needs defining. (To find out about SMART principles go to Chapter 5.)

- Should I be following my intuition? *Yes*, because my record of what I did before is stored in the shed and it's freezing today, so I'm not going outside to check!

- Do I want to get motivated for the task? *Yes.*

- What's stopping my motivation? *Winter* – it's freezing!

- Am I more motivated in some areas of my life than others, for example, putting my family before work? *No.*

- What is going to help me feel motivated right now? *Spring time.*

- What has helped me stay motivated in the past that can benefit me now? *Starting* my task. It was easier than I anticipated.

- Am I looking to become more motivated in order to have a more positive outlook about life in general? *Not applicable* in this case.

Setting yourself a specific and realistic timescale for the start and ending of a task helps you to avoid creating a deadline that you can't possibly achieve. For example, if you have to get your children off to school and do other essential jobs early in the morning, telling yourself that you're going to start at 10:30 am rather than 9:00 am gives you a better chance of achieving your goal.

In Table 9-2, you have the opportunity to readjust and raise your personal motivation score after considering the questions in the preceding section. For example, you may want to up your score by giving more weight to rewards or the importance of the task.

Table 9-2	Raising My Personal Motivation Score	
Motivational area	*What am I hoping to achieve by completing my task?*	*Score for each motivational area* *1 = Not motivated* *10 = Highly motivated*
Importance	A sense of achievement?	
Reward	Getting a reward – intrinsic or extrinsic – that is going to benefit me? (Refer to Chapter 8 for more on intrinsic and extrinsic rewards.)	
Feel-good factor	Feeling positive and good about myself?	
Benefit to others	Benefit other people?	
Focus	Gives me the opportunity to focus on other areas of my life?	
Easy to do	Easy to achieve, taking little effort?	
Time-saving	Keeping a record of how I went about the task is going to save time overall and helps me to work more efficiently?	
Counting the cost	Avoiding paying a fine or penalty?	
Optional additional area depending on the task		

The areas where you give yourself higher scores show that you're well motivated and on target for completing your task in that particular area. In those areas where you have a low score, you need to find ways of increasing your motivation to achieve your overall goal.

Exploring the Brain

Your brain is the main organ of the central nervous system and home to your thinking, speech, sensation, motion, memory, and imagination. The way the brain works affects how you interpret situations and experiences, and how motivated you feel when facing a task or challenge.

The thoughts in your brain and how you process information can affect how motivated you feel. Each area of the brain is responsible for different actions and processes information in different ways. Understanding how the brain works can help unlock some of the reasons why you could feel more or less motivated to do something.

If you're someone who likes to understand how something works, understanding the workings of the brain and which parts of it affect your behaviour will be important to you.

Figure 9-1 shows the three main parts of the brain. Here's what those three parts actually do:

- **Brain stem:** Sometimes called the reptilian brain, referring to the first stages of evolution. This area of the brain is responsible for keeping you awake and alert, controlling breathing, heart rate, and sleeping patterns. The brain stem contains the reticular activating system (RAS), which controls consciousness. The brain stem also detects incoming sensory information and relays signals through the mid-brain to the cerebral cortex.

- **Limbic brain (mid-brain):** This area of the brain contains several parts including the hypothalamus, hippocampus, and amygdala. The amygdala, is important for memory and emotions. The whole area of the limbic is vital for long-term memory function and helps control your emotions, sexuality, and instinctive behaviour, such as the flight-or-fight stress responses (including anger and fear). The hypothalamus, together with the pituitary gland, helps regulate body temperature, food intake, water–salt balance, the sleep–wake cycle, and the activity of hormones.

- **Cerebral cortex:** Also called the left and right cerebral hemispheres. The cerebral cortex is your 'thinking cap', because it helps to process sensory information – seeing, hearing, speech, and touch. The cerebral cortex also controls intellectual processes: reasoning and thinking. Both sides of the cerebral cortex are important for processing incoming data, but each side of the cerebral cortex processes information differently.

If you have the gift of being able to use both sides of the cerebral cortex simultaneously, keeping motivated is often easier because you're more likely to come up with creative ways of keeping on track. You see around problems or how to jump over hurdles to find a way of moving forward toward your goal.

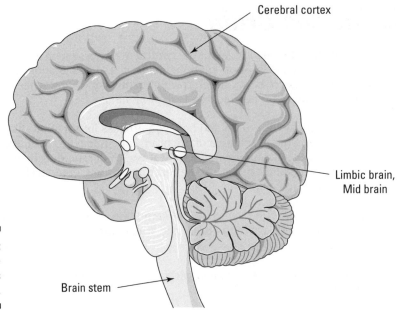

Cerebral cortex

Limbic brain,
Mid brain

Brain stem

Figure 9-1:
The three
main parts
of the brain.

Different sides, different processes

Figure 9-2 shows how the left side and the right side of the brain process different types of information and produce different ideas. The key to using your brain effectively, absorbing information, and increasing performance is having the ability to use both sides of the brain at the same time, increasing the number of connections between brain cells.

Your brain contains roughly 100 billion brain cells. The more you stimulate your brain cells the more you encourage new connections and new pathways. Brain research suggests that the number of connections determines intelligence.

Perhaps you're in the habit of always travelling the same way to work or parking in the same place in the car park? The more you do the same thing over and over again, the more your brain cells are programmed to repeat the action until it becomes second nature. If you occasionally take an alternative route or park in a different place, you stimulate your brain cells and prevent your brain from continuing the habit.

Have a go at challenging your brain by doing things in a different way from time to time. This helps the left side and the right side of your brain to work together to create new solutions to problems, stimulates new connections, and increases your number of brain cells.

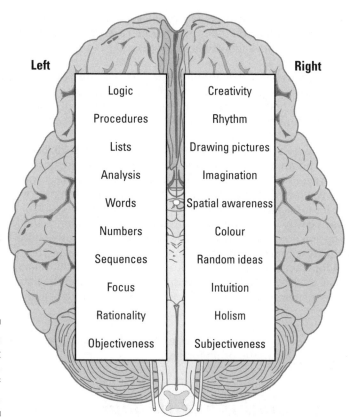

Left   Right

Logic	Creativity
Procedures	Rhythm
Lists	Drawing pictures
Analysis	Imagination
Words	Spatial awareness
Numbers	Colour
Sequences	Random ideas
Focus	Intuition
Rationality	Holism
Objectiveness	Subjectiveness

Figure 9-2:
The right
side and the
left side of
the brain.

Try cleaning your teeth holding your toothbrush in your non-dominant hand for a few days. Your bathroom will, no doubt, soon be covered in toothpaste! However, after a few days you find that you begin to feel more comfortable as you develop your new habit. You need to repeat a new habit 21 times to develop a different brain pathway or neural connection.

Recognising the differences between sexes

Many of you know only too well that men and women approach life from quite different angles! This is because men and women often use one side of the brain more than the other. Women tend to be more verbal, using twice as many words as men. In contrast, men are more non-verbal, often preferring action to talking. Men and women can have quite different priorities: the sexes differ in what's important and what motivates them to work well.

Often men are more motivated by a project that gives them power and control and are happy working on their own. Women are frequently more emotionally driven and happy working with another person or in a team.

Men are likely to jump straight into a project without bothering with the finer details, whereas women usually ask a lot of questions to make sure that they understand the task. I am generalising, but employers should be aware of the differences when trying to motivate members of their team.

The area between the left side and the right side of the brain is called the corpus callosum. This area of the brain is made of nerve fibres connecting specific areas of the two cerebral hemispheres together. The width of the corpus callosum differs between men and women. It is slightly wider (or thicker!) in women, making it easier for messages to pass from the left side to the right side of the brain. That may be why women find multitasking easy, being able to think of more than one thing at a time. Men process information predominantly on the left side of the brain. Research carried out on London taxi drivers bears this out. Taxi drivers (predominantly men) learn *The Knowledge* as lists of information, (using the left side of the brain). However, taxi drivers then interpret the data by creating pictures and images (using the right side of their brain) to help them memorise the routes.

But don't forget, *both* men and women have the capacity to stimulate and develop each side of the brain further.

Are you thinking with your left side or right side?

Tackle the Brain Dominance Questionnaire in Table 9-3 to find out whether you have a preference for using the left side or right side of your brain. Before you begin, write down the numbers 1 to 15. As you go through the questionnaire, select A or B, depending on which statement relates to you. Choose a statement, even if your preference is very slight.

Table 9-3	Brain Dominance Questionnaire	
Question number	*Brain dominance questions*	*Circle A or B*
1.	A. It's fun to take risks. B. I have fun without taking risks.	A/B

Question number	Brain dominance questions	Circle A or B
2.	A. I look for new ways of doing old jobs. B. When one way works well, I don't change it.	A/B
3.	A. I begin a lot of jobs that I never finish. B. I finish a job before starting a new one.	A/B
4.	A. I'm not very imaginative in my work. B. I use my imagination in everything I do.	A/B
5.	A. I can analyse what is going to happen next. B. I can sense what is going to happen next.	A/B
6.	A. I try to find just one way of solving a problem. B. I try to find different answers to a problem.	A/B
7.	A. My thinking is like pictures going through my head. B. My thinking is like words going through my head.	A/B
8.	A. I am always the first person to take on board new ideas. B. I question new ideas more than other people do.	A/B
9.	A. People don't see me as a good organiser. B. Other people think I organise well.	A/B
10.	A. I have a lot of self-discipline. B. I usually act on my gut feelings.	A/B
11.	A. I plan time for doing my work. B. I don't think about the time when I work.	A/B
12.	A. With a hard decision, I choose what I know is right. B. With a hard decision, I choose what I feel is right.	A/B

(continued)

Table 9-3: *(continued)*

Question number	Brain dominance questions	Circle A or B
13.	A. I do the easy things first and important things later. B. I do the important things first and the easy things later.	A/B
14.	A. Sometimes in a new situation, I have too many ideas. B. Sometimes in a new situation, I don't have any ideas.	A/B
15.	A. I like to have change and variety in my life. B. I like an orderly and well-planned life.	A/B

Source: The Alert Scale of Cognition, by Dr Loren D. Crane (1989).

To find your total score:

- Give yourself *one* point for each time you answered *A* to questions 1, 2, 3, 7, 8, 9, 13, 14, 15
- Give yourself *one* point for each time you answered *B* to questions 4, 5, 6, 10, 11, 12

Add your points together and then compare your total score with the scores in Table 9-4 to find out how the left side and right side of your brain are working for you.

Table 9-4	Key to Your Brain Dominance
Score	*Brain dominance*
0–3 points	Strong left brain
4–6 points	Moderate left brain
7–9 points	Equally left and right focus
10–12 points	Moderate right brain
13–15 points	Strong right brain

Source: The Alert Scale of Cognition, by Dr Loren D. Crane (1989).

Connecting to both sides

To stimulate and develop your brain and to connect to both sides, or to develop the least strong side of your brain, you need to tell your brain you want it to perform in new ways.

The following are ways of connecting to both sides of your brain:

- Performing exercises (see 'Understanding brain gym and desk exercises' sidebar)
- Talking to people to stimulate ideas
- Playing ball games with your non-dominant hand
- Writing your name with your non-dominant hand
- Brushing your teeth with your non-dominant hand
- Drinking plenty of water – dehydration or thirst can impair the neural pathways to the brain. Sipping water slowly and frequently helps your concentration, alertness, speed of reactions, and also helps fight fatigue.

Ways of stimulating the right side of your brain:

- Daydreaming
- Taking a break
- Stimulating your senses; for example, watching a film, visiting an art gallery, listening to music
- Walking or exercise
- Taking up a hobby

Ways of stimulating the left side of your brain:

- Following a recipe step by step
- Using satellite navigation when driving, rather than finding your way by instinct
- Memorising your 12 times table
- Doing a crossword, Sudoku, or playing chess

Understanding brain gym and desk exercises

These exercises are simple to do, take only a few minutes, and can give you a new lease of life. You can try doing them at any time of the day, in between projects, on your own or with friends. These exercises increase the blood supply and oxygen to your brain, boosting your energy. They release stress and tension caused by sitting in one position for a long time (for example, when you're working on a computer). They can also increase the flow of happy hormones (endorphins) to make you feel good.

Warning: Take care if you have a neck, back, or shoulder injury if you're thinking of doing the brain gym and desk exercises.

Desk exercises (designed by The Chartered Society of Physiotherapy)

1. **Place your hands behind your head, gently flaring both elbows out to the side of your body.**

2. **Shrug your shoulders up and down to release tension.**

3. **Circle shoulders forwards and backwards.**

4. **Stand up, stretching your arms out to the side of your body to form a T-junction and gently circle both arms backwards and then forwards.**

Brain gym

Brain gym exercises were developed in the late 1980s by Drs Dennison and Dennison for children with learning difficulties. The series of exercises helps to stimulate brain activity and, in particular, improve whole-brain learning. The exercises are now used widely with adults and children to enhance creativity, learning, reading, thinking, and memory. Doing the brain gym exercises helps to energise you and gives your eyes the rest they need from computer work. Check out these exercises:

- **Cross crawl:** Stand up and, with your right hand, touch your left knee. With your left hand, touch your right knee and then repeat the exercise several times. You can also try variations using your elbow to your knee or taking your hand behind you to the opposite heel (backward variation). This exercise stimulates creativity and improves concentration because the arm and leg exercises cross over the midline of the body.

- **Lazy 8 or elephant trunk:** Using your right hand, draw a sideways figure of eight in the air as if your arm was like a long trunk. Then use the left arm to do the same, allowing your eyes to follow your hand movements so that your eyes cross your visual midline. This exercise relaxes neck muscles and improves your listening skills and balance.

- **Hook-ups:** Sit down and extend your arms in front of you. Cross your left wrist over your right, interlace your fingers, and draw your hands up towards your chest. Sitting in this position, breathe with your eyes closed to help you relax. A variation is crossing your legs and arms. Cross your left leg over your right and your right hand over your left and relax in that position before changing over. This exercise helps you feel relaxed but at the same time energised and attentive.

Practising Motivational Exercises

Motivational exercises are designed to boost your energy and enthusiasm, help your breathing, and make you feel more relaxed. The exercises can be done on your own or in a group. Performing the exercises with a group can help to strengthen relationships, build understanding, and get people working together in harmony.

During your working day you spend a lot of time using the left side of your brain: like following processes and procedures. Motivational exercises stimulate the right side of the brain, improving your motivation, confidence, developing initiative, and unleashing creativity. Exercises stimulating the right side of your brain can take you out of your comfort zone, but bring you a different outlook on life, which can be the key to unlocking barriers to your motivation.

Doing motivational exercises gives you the chance of coming up against new and different situations not normally part of your day-to-day experience – for example, team working or acquiring a new skill. Bringing together employees, managers, and bosses to practise the motivational exercises is a good way of removing barriers and encouraging cohesiveness.

Activities to try

Physical activities can be fun and relaxing as well as helping you build up your motivation. Some people are very happy to take part, whereas other people can be put off by the idea of joining in and performing. Individuals have different strengths, weaknesses, and preferences, which need to be taken into account when working with motivational exercises. But physically experiencing a situation rather than just reading or hearing about it can pay dividends.

Get moving and try some of the following activities and exercises.

Alternative juggling in a group of people
Dan Collins from Fresh Tracks (see the Appendix for more details) uses the following exercise, included here with permission.

Before starting the exercise you first need a load of bean bags, enough for two for each participant. If you don't have bean bags you can use juggling balls instead or even packets of sweets! No physical ability in juggling is required!

1. **In groups of three, each person is given one bean bag. On a count of three you throw the bean bag to the person on your left at the same time as they catch the bean bag from the person on their right.**

   At this stage you are going to be in fits of laughter as most of the bean bags land on the floor completely missing your hands.

   After several attempts and good team work you are delighted at having achieved a clear round. It's interesting to see the different strategies for success that each group adopts.

2. **You can challenge each group further by asking them to change direction or to join with another group so that they make up six people in larger circles simultaneously juggling bean bags.**

3. **When each person masters throwing and catching one bean bag, the next stage is to give each person two bean bags and repeat the exercise. This time you're throwing one bag from your right to your left hand and one bag from your left to your neighbour's right hand, and simultaneously (hopefully!) catching two bean bags from the person on your right.**

   By this time the exercise should have achieved its aim of everyone having a good laugh, breaking down the barriers, and helping those taking part to have a 'can do' or 'want to do' attitude for the rest of the day!

Coordination, mutual support, and pin-sharp timing are needed to succeed at this challenge. It takes a bit of time to get the hang of juggling but when it goes right you feel elated and the achievement is unforgettable. It's a powerful and effective team exercise.

Of course you can also learn to juggle on your own. A bonus is that a minute of juggling three balls is equivalent to 200 throws of the ball, the equivalent of lifting over 20 kilos of weights in a gym.

I often build juggling exercises into the training courses I run. Some participants, initially, aren't happy with the idea of juggling. However, as the day progresses and they have a bit of time to practise, it's lovely to see people improve as they acquire the new skill. The 'I can't do it' from the morning is replaced with 'I am nearly there' in the afternoon. Facing the challenge of mastering something new helps in building self-confidence.

Listening to music

Music can have the effect of increasing your brain activity, and brain waves in particular. Music with a faster beat (more than 80 beats per minute) often makes you feel more awake and alert than slower, relaxing music (under 60 beats per minute) does. Music helps in motivational exercises, such as juggling, because people tend to listen to the music, helping to take away their potential fear of learning a new skill or doing a group activity. Certain pieces of music encourage individuals to sing along in their head or to feel good. Do you have a favourite piece of uplifting music?

Jump back to Chapter 3 for more about using music to motivate you.

Giving feedback and saying thank you

This is one of the simplest exercises but one people often find surprisingly hard to do. Saying 'well done' can have a powerful motivating effect, translating as 'you are doing really well, well done, let's have another go'.

Breaking the rules

Encouraging activities that don't follow strict rules and procedures is refreshing and motivating. Getting people to wander around the room or office as if they were at a cocktail party and stopping to chat to different people is a useful brainstorming exercise and great for capturing new ideas.

Drawing pictures

This activity uses the right side of the brain and, if carried out in small groups of people, can be very effective. Give each group 5 to 10 minutes to draw a picture of a motivated person and a non-motivated person. Using coloured scented pens brings your senses of seeing and smelling into play, as well as enhancing the characteristics of the people in the drawings. Each group presents and talks through their picture at the end of the activity.

Role-playing

This is another activity that is particularly good for developing the right side of the brain, as it encourages you to use your imagination. Place people in small groups and ask them to act out how a motivated and non-motivated person behave. Acting lets you experience many different emotions, increasing your understanding of what other people are thinking and feeling.

Enjoying the fresh air

Taking a walk in the fresh air on a sunny day is a wonderful energiser as well as an excellent form of exercise. The lift you get after returning from your walk motivates you to return to the task at hand with renewed enthusiasm. If your work doesn't allow you time off for walking outdoors, leaving your desk and walking round the building or your office serves the same purpose.

Following a simple exercise routine

You can benefit from doing even simple exercises. Using your favourite exercise DVD, taking a few moments to have a go at the latest Wii fitness activity, running up and down the stairs or around the garden to wake you up, throwing the ball for the dog, putting on your favourite disco dance music and dancing wildly to your favourite song are all good examples of using exercise to boost your energy and enthusiasm.

Taking a break

Stop for a drink, have a snack, or even read the paper! The action of stopping what you're doing and taking a break can often remotivate you. A power nap or a 20-minute meditation, for example, can recharge your mind, increase your energy levels, and give your body a break.

Motivational quotations

We can often get a boost from listening to the wisdom of those who had more than their share of brain cells! Here are just a handful of motivational quotations from people who achieved great things.

We cannot solve our problems with the same level of thinking that created them. (Albert Einstein)

It is amazing what you can accomplish if you do not care who gets the credit. (US President Harry S Truman)

In the midst of winter, I finally learned that within me there lay an invincible summer. (Albert Camus, 1913–1960, French author and philosopher)

A dream is just a dream. A goal is a dream with a plan and a deadline. (Harvey Mackay)

I have learned that success is to be measured not so much by the position that one has reached in life as by the obstacles overcome while trying to succeed. (Booker T Washington, 1856–1915)

Most people never run far enough on their first wind to find out they've got a second.

Give your dreams all you've got and you'll be amazed at the energy that comes out of you. (William James, American Psychologist and Philosopher, 1842–1910)

Whatever you can do – or dream you can do – begin it. Boldness has genius, power, and magic in it. (Johann Wolfgang von Goethe, German writer, 1749–1832)

A dwarf standing on the shoulders of a giant may see farther than the giant himself. (Didacus Stella, circa AD 60 – and, as a matter of interest, abridged on the edge of an English £2 coin)

If I have seen further it is by standing on the shoulders of giants. (Sir Isaac Newton, 1676)

The most important thing in life is not to capitalise on your successes – any fool can do that. The really important thing is to profit from your mistakes. (William Bolitho, from Twelve against the Gods)

People often say that motivation doesn't last. Well, neither does bathing. That's why we recommend it daily. (Zig Ziglar)

Visualisation: Experiencing the future

Visualisation is a way of using all your senses to mentally rehearse a future event and picture a positive outcome. You bring your imagination into play, which is an effective way of stimulating and developing the right side of your brain. Head to Chapter 6 for a full description of the techniques of visualisation.

Stepping into motivation

Getting yourself motivated takes courage. You need to be bold and prepared to step out of your comfort zone. Stepping forward into motivation often involves taking risks, making mistakes, and feeling a bit scared, but the rewards can be worth the effort.

Tricking your brain into believing you are well motivated can help you move forward confidently. Simply the action of starting the task gives you the momentum to take that first step forward and on and upwards to the next step.

Chapter 10

Using Neuro-linguistic Programming as a Motivating Tool

. . . .

In This Chapter

▶ Deciding what drives you forward

▶ Interpreting what's going on in your head

▶ Understanding your inactivity

. . . .

*I*n this chapter, I help you understand how you can use Neuro-linguistic Programming to build up your motivation. You also take a journey through the logical levels and identify the possible by-products of deciding not to do anything!

Just What Is Neuro-linguistic Programming?

Neuro-linguistic Programming (NLP) has been around since the late 1970s. It is an alternative therapy where you programme the brain to improve your self-awareness, giving you the ability to plan and reach your goal. You model your behaviour on successful people and develop your communication skills to help you gain rapport.

NLP is used worldwide and can apply to every aspect of your personal and professional life. NLP was developed by a group of psychologists, psycho-therapists, linguists, and anthropologists. The group identified different styles of language, highlighted brain patterns, and sequences of behaviour. Armed with their findings the group developed the NLP techniques used today.

Here's how NLP breaks down:

- *Neuro* concerns your brain and what's happening in your mind.
- *Linguistic* refers to language and what you say.
- *Programming* refers to patterns of behaviour that you study and copy.

You can explore the use of NLP in much greater detail in *Neuro-linguistic Programming For Dummies* and the *Neuro-linguistic Programming Workbook For Dummies*, both by Romilla Ready and Kate Burton (Wiley).

Finding Out What Makes You Tick

Knowing what makes you tick is useful for understanding your behaviour, your actions, or even your inaction. It also helps in deciding which aspects of motivation will be more effective for you. So what does make you tick? Is it something inside you or something outside, driving you forward? Here are a few replies I've had to my question:

- Striving for success
- Wanting to achieve
- Being better than my friends
- Wanting to prove myself
- Knowing there is going to be a reward
- Fear of failure
- Not wanting to be left out
- Wanting to do good
- Giving people a valuable service
- Travelling and appreciating different cultures
- Gaining power
- Exploring new possibilities

Some people find it hard to put into words what makes them tick, while others can describe what makes them tick in great detail.

Using the senses in motivation

A key feature of NLP is interpreting situations around you by using your five senses:

- ✔ **Seeing:** Visual people prefer information that is presented in diagrams or in pictures. Try playing about with a picture in your mind: making it larger or smaller, increasing or decreasing the brightness and contrast, or adding movement. Compare adjusting the picture in your mind to using a zoom lens going in closer or further away from the object, getting a close-up or a wide-angled view.

- ✔ **Hearing:** The sounds you hear such as voices and music. The tone of someone's voice allows you to interpret what the person is saying and meaning. Imagine yourself turning up the volume, regulating the pitch and rhythm. You can also experiment with hearing sounds in mono, stereo, or quadraphonics.

- ✔ **Feeling:** Experiencing a feeling, intuition, or instinct. You can experience the sensuous feel of velvet or crisp new sheets against your skin, the impact of a hug or a meaningful handshake. You can imagine feeling hot or cold, and degrees of heat and coldness. You can also have feelings of happiness, joy and pleasure, or feelings of sorrow and sadness.

- ✔ **Taste:** Responses linked to food and drink. For example, being aware how taste affects your palate: sweet, sour, sharp, savoury, hot, spicy, or bitter.

- ✔ **Smell/aroma:** Your sense of smell is linked to mood and memories. Smells travel faster to the limbic area of the brain than your other senses. A smell or aroma can evoke an emotional response, triggering the memory of a previous experience; like the first time you wore your favourite perfume or an aftershave lotion reminding you of your first boyfriend.

Your senses help to explain the meaning of what's going on around you, the way you're communicating, and how you're recording events.

Everyone interprets a situation slightly differently. You may enjoy the smell of freshly mown grass, while another person gets most pleasure out of seeing the neat and tidy garden. The sensory stimulus occurs outside your body (or, in other words, the view you look at is outside the body), but the processing takes place inside and is registered in the brain through the optic nerve, creating different interpretations of the world around you.

You can strengthen your motivation by bringing your senses into play. Using the visualisation techniques described in Chapter 6, you can fine-tune your senses further. Imagine you are turning up the volume on your music player to hear the music more loudly; in a similar way you can turn up the volume and intensity of your feelings, so heightening your emotional responses.

Sensory awareness is being conscious of your surroundings. For example, what you notice when you walk into a building, office, or house for the first time. Do you hear the sounds and voices of people or the clock ticking? Are you having good vibes or does the building seem forbidding? Do you sense that the people living or working there are happy or subdued? Are you taking in the pictures on the walls, the colour of the paintwork, the furnishings?

Once during a training course, I asked a participant to describe her home to me. She had no idea what colour the walls in her apartment were painted, but she knew how she felt about living there. The apartment made little visual impact on her, but it always felt welcoming and relaxing, and was the place she enjoyed living in with her partner. Clearly she had a strongly developed sense of feeling, but her visual sense was much less dominant.

Exploring the senses in more detail

Making use of the visualisation techniques in Chapter 6 you can boost your motivation to achieve your goal by taking the following steps:

1. **Picture your goal in your mind.**

   Intensify the image by changing the black and white picture to full colour, and giving the image action by making the still into a movie, and putting yourself in as the lead character.

2. **Bring more sounds and voices into the scene.**

   Hear people praise you and make positive comments as you achieve your goal, and imagine hearing the sound of an audience clapping and cheering.

3. **Work up the intensity of your feelings as you imagine experiencing the sensation of achieving your goal.**

   Some people experience a positive feeling in their body as they imagine achieving their goal. They can feel the sensation in their chest, heart, or deep down inside their stomach.

   You can experience the heavy, cool, and smooth feeling of the Oscar in your hands, the feeling as you burst through the tape at the end of the marathon, or how you feel inside when you receive the standing ovation or vote of thanks.

4. **If your senses of taste and smell have a part to play in achieving your goal, enhance your visualisation by bringing them into the scene.**

Looking at the other person's point of view

It's no surprise to find that many people you meet have quite a different view of the world from yourself or see the same situation in an entirely different light. This is evident in many aspects of your personal or working life. For example, you ask someone to do something, only to be surprised that they tackle the task in a completely different way to you. Your view or 'map of the world' isn't necessarily the same as the other person's map of the world. Your way of looking at things is important, but being able to see the other person's point of view plays an important part in motivation and communicating well.

As an example, you may enjoy keeping your home organised and tidy so you can always find things. Alternatively, your neighbour could have a very different approach, with possessions strewn everywhere. You both have different maps of the world about what is important in your home and how you manage and organise things.

Accepting each person's own map of the world is important, otherwise you could tend towards imposing seemingly rigid views on someone else. This would affect your ability to communicate effectively and possibly also their motivation.

Enhancing visualisation

Sean's goal was to improve his golf. In his mind, he pictured himself playing the perfect round. To enhance his picture, he visualised walking around the golf course and playing each hole. He saw each hole clearly, where he was playing from, the surrounding area, and the condition of the green and fairway.

He saw himself swinging his club and hitting each ball successfully. In his mind's eye, he could see his accurate putt dropping the ball in the hole.

Sean also focused on what he was thinking and saying and what advice the golf pro was giving him. He imagined hearing the praise after playing a good round. He then focused on his feelings, relaxing his body, and moving freely getting the full length to his stroke. He thought back to when he last felt confident on the golf course, intensifying the feeling, seeing himself as strong and confident.

Sean had fine-tuned his senses of seeing, hearing, and feeling to a pitch that inspired and motivated him to go out and play a brilliant round of golf.

If your map of the world stops you doing something, such as flying, it may be problematic and could limit what you're able to do and how motivated you are to try something different, such as visiting a new country. However, in most situations, your personal map of the world is as valid as anyone else's map.

I remember being shown how to finely chop onions. Later on, when I saw someone chopping onions using a different method, I thought they had it all wrong, until I realised there are more ways than one to chop onions finely! As long as the technique works, it doesn't matter which method you choose if you get the result you want.

How other people are thinking and behaving can have a powerful effect on your motivation, in both positive and negative ways. Working alongside a person who is cheerful and has a positive attitude to the job can boost your motivation, whereas being with someone who's unhappy and demoralised can be soulless and demotivating.

Be open to chance comments from people and work what you hear and see to your advantage. Another person's perspective can trigger fresh ideas and new approaches, motivating you onwards and upwards towards your goal.

I was setting up a training course recently and I asked for an extension lead. My client asked me how long I wanted it. My response was that I needed the extension lead for the whole day. It so happened that my client was asking his question from an entirely different perspective to mine. His question was how long in *metres* did the lead need to be! We both arrived at the right answer, but having approached the question from a different perspective.

A friend of mine runs a business with two fellow directors. Anna always arrives at important meetings clutching a huge box file bursting with ill-assorted documents. Pierre, the ex-accountant, arrives with a neatly partitioned red folder with the key information required for the meeting carefully sorted. Simon, the ideas man, usually dashes in late with no paper, pen, or documents, asking Anna if she can lend him pen and paper. Each has a valuable role to play in the company but approach critical meetings from an entirely different stand.

Exploring Logical Levels

Logical levels are the brain-child of Robert Dilts, an NLP trainer. The logical levels are a way of getting a grip on what you're thinking, helping you to readjust the balance in your life, and deal with changes. Each logical level can help you to identify what is stopping you from succeeding and explains where your motivation is coming from. You can explore logical levels further in *Neuro-linguistic Programming For Dummies*.

Figure 10-1 illustrates the five logical levels, with an optional sixth level depending on the context. Those levels are:

- ✔ **Environment:** The environment refers to your surroundings. Where you need to be working, what you physically need, who you need around you, the time of the day. Having all these conditions in place helps to motivate you to achieve your goal. For example, just moving to a more comfortable desk or quieter work area to cut out distractions can help make your task easier and more straightforward.

- ✔ **Behaviour:** Behaviour is what you actually do, the actions you need to take to achieve your goal. Lack of motivation at this logical level is about what is happening or what is being done.

- ✔ **Capability:** How capable you are of achieving your goal and your confidence in your ability to do it. Do you have the skills and knowledge to carry out the task? Do you have the resources you need? Do you need extra training, knowledge, or skills to help you move forward?

- ✔ **Beliefs and values:** Do you believe the goal or task is right for you? This logical level takes into account your personal beliefs or values in relation to your task or goal. Beliefs can include whether your task is ethical, safe, or if it's going to benefit other people. You can choose not to take action if the task does not satisfy your beliefs, for example, being a vegetarian or a pacifist.

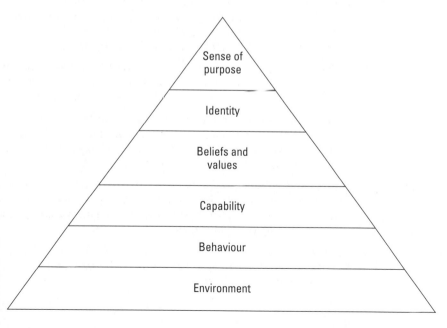

Figure 10-1:
Logical
levels.

✔ **Identity:** This logical level is linked to your self-confidence and self-esteem. For example, do you believe that reaching your goal is going to make a difference to your career and your future?

✔ **Sense of purpose:** Having a sense of purpose is about where you see yourself in the world and your mission in life, like wanting to care for sick people or doing voluntary work in newly developing countries. Having a strong sense of purpose is likely to mean you are already highly motivated.

Exploring your responses to each logical level can help you identify barriers, make changes, and boost your motivation.

Bear in mind that trying to boost your motivation in relation to your sense of identity is the most difficult logical level to tackle. For example, you can change your environment by moving to another room relatively easily, but changing how you feel related to your self-confidence and esteem may take longer. However, when your identity is clear, you're often happy to march ahead. Unfortunately, if you have a distorted sense of your own identity, for better or worse, this can lead you to march ahead in the wrong direction. Taking time to focus on your true identity is time well spent.

Imagine you have set yourself the goal of finding a new job; then link your goal to each of the logical levels.

✔ **Environment:** Do you need to cut down on commuting and find a job nearer home or in another part of the country? Do you need to look for a new job now or can you afford to spend time researching job possibilities? Do you prefer working in a small company with few staff or with a big organisation and working with many colleagues? Ask yourself specific questions about *where*, *when*, and *with whom* your new job should be.

✔ **Behaviour:** What type of work do you want to do? What activities are you going to be engaged in on a day-to-day basis? Ask yourself questions related to your specific *actions* and *what* you want to do.

✔ **Capability:** Do you need to gain new skills and knowledge? Do you need to do further study to gain more qualifications allowing you to make a career change? Ask yourself questions about *how* your present skills and capabilities are suitable for that new job.

✔ **Beliefs and values:** Do you believe you are ready for and deserve promotion? Is the new job going to match your personal values and beliefs? Is the job likely to reinforce what you believe in? Asking yourself questions about *why* you want the job is important.

✔ **Identity:** Will the job give you a strong sense of identity? Is the job going to enhance your self-image? Ask yourself the question *who* am I and how does my sense of self fit the job?

✔ **Sense of Purpose:** Will the job satisfy your overall goal in life and what you want to achieve? Do you feel passionate about the job and will it help you achieve your mission in life?

As you explore each logical level make sure you ask the specific questions, *where*, *when*, and *with whom*, *what*, *how*, and *why*. This approach shows you which areas you need to work on to increase your motivation to get that new job.

If you want to identify the changes you need to make to achieve your goal ask yourself:

✔ Where do I need to be? (Environment)

✔ When do I want the new job? (Environment)

✔ Who do I want to work with and in what kind of business or profession? (Environment)

✔ What specific actions do I need to take to get a new job? (Behaviour)

✔ How's this job playing to my strengths? (Capability)

✔ Why do I want to change? (Beliefs and values)

✔ Does this job fit in with my sense of self? (Identity)

✔ Is the change going help my purpose in life? (Purpose)

✔ How does the new job benefit me? (Purpose)

Identifying the Positive By-Products of Inactivity

Positive by-products are what you gain, often subconsciously, from how you're behaving at the moment or simply by not acting at all. (For much more on positive by-products go to Chapter 4.) A positive by-product can occur if you are unable to make changes, aren't motivated to change because you are happy with your current situation (although you may not realise it), or you believe there's some benefit or pay-off from staying as you are.

Examples of inactivity include putting things off, making excuses, only doing the easy jobs, not making time for the task, and not giving the task enough importance.

Positive by-products at work

A friend of mine was telling me about his brother, Hamish, who was seeing a business coach. Hamish was working in central London as a salesman. He had moved to London from a poor area of Glasgow, his home town, to be with his girlfriend. Hamish was being helped by a coach because he felt he lacked the motivation to perform his job to his full potential. He earned a basic salary, which could be considerably enhanced on a commission basis depending on the number of telephone sales he made. For reasons he couldn't fathom, Hamish found he lacked the motivation to make the necessary number of calls, and he was now facing the prospect of getting a very poor performance review and certainly no bonus this year. Both Hamish and his coach were puzzled as to why Hamish lacked the motivation to do a job that previously, up in Glasgow, he had been very good at, and that promised to pay a high salary.

In order to understand at what level the problem arose, Hamish's coach took him through the logical levels. Firstly, thinking about the environment, Hamish said he had his own office from which to make these calls. It was comfortable and suited him well. This was not the level from which his lack of motivation arose. The next logical level, behaviour, didn't seem to be the problem either. Hamish enjoyed making cold calls and talking on the phone. The third level, capability, was definitely not where the issue lay because at his previous company Hamish had won the salesman of the year award for the most sales made by cold calling. His beliefs and values were not violated because Hamish believed in his company's product and was aware of its benefits from the people who bought it.

It became obvious to Hamish's coach that Hamish's lack of motivation arose from an issue relating to Hamish's identity. In some way, Hamish's sense of self was being challenged. It took several coaching sessions for Hamish to realise that he still saw himself as a working-class boy from Scotland, with strong socialist principles, and a very highly developed resistance to what he deemed to be the trappings of capitalism. He knew that if he made enough telesales he was in a position to earn a very substantial salary. But if he had a large salary, how could he still be that working-class boy who scorned capitalism? In other words, Hamish no longer knew who he was.

Of course, Hamish's identity crisis wasn't rearing its head at a conscious level. But the positive by-product of not performing well in his new job, and not making enough calls, even though he enjoyed making them and was a very good salesman, was that he did not have to face the dilemma inside him of who he was now. Was he still the boy from a working-class family in Glasgow, or was he an affluent Londoner now able to afford the best that the London social scene had to offer?

My friend told me that his brother continued to work with his coach until they found a way of allowing Hamish to be successful in his job, and accept the salary and rewards that being successful brings. Hamish has come to terms with his dilemma by giving away some of his wealth, usually to charity, and so staying true to his socialist principles.

Sometimes doing nothing brings its own rewards. By not taking a particular action you may find yourself taking a route that you had not even considered before, opening up new opportunities and being more productive in the long run. Your inactivity can also highlight the current level of your motivation and whether you need to address this before taking further action to achieve your goal.

Try using the positive by-products from your inactive state as a tool for making much-needed changes. To identify your positive by-products ask yourself:

- What's my behaviour doing for me?
- What's my inaction helping me do instead?
- What do I get out of my current situation?
- Is anything else affected directly or indirectly by my not taking action?
- Which elements are worth keeping?
- Is my current behaviour helping other people?

After you've identified the positive by-product ask 'How can I get this benefit elsewhere or in another way?'

Positive by-products are often buried deep in your subconscious. You may need the help of a coach or other professional to help you dig them out. Meanwhile, use Table 10-1 to identify positive by-products of not taking action in your present situation.

Table 10-1	Identifying Positive By-Products	
Aspect of your behaviour	*What is the possible positive by-product of your behaviour?*	*How is the positive by-product helping you or other people?* *(This can relate to an individual or a department at work.)*
For example: Inaction: putting things off, unwilling to make changes, or make decisions		

Changing your mind!

A friend of mine was working for a major European company. The company had offices throughout Europe employing many nationalities (English, French, Italian, German, Polish, Spanish, and Belgian). English was the main language spoken within the company. However, as a way of integrating the staff, language classes were being offered in the lunchtime break.

My friend was highly motivated to learn a new language and immediately enrolled in the first class. I saw her the next day and asked how she got on and was very surprised when she said that she was dropping out. She explained that the German class she went to had a lot of people in it who had studied German before, so she felt left behind.

She didn't allow the setback to put her off her desire of learning a language and she enrolled the next day in the Italian class instead, where everyone was at a similar level. She felt happy with her decision and looked forward to going to Italy to practise her new language skills.

Now, take the story of Tanvir. He had been working for a large organisation for several years. Every couple of years he had the opportunity to move to different departments to gain more management experience. He worked within teams, learning about interviewing and recruitment, performance appraisals, and general team management. At the same time he was doing an Open University management course to build on his experience and also gain a qualification.

The company ran a Trainee General Manager Programme. Tanvir decided to apply for the programme, which lead to managing a division of 100 plus people. After the interview he was offered a place on the programme, which initially accepted and then declined.

Tanvir realised he preferred working on his own or with small groups of people, rather than overseeing a large division. The experience he had gained from the Trainee General Manager Programme had been invaluable, but having the job of a general manager looking after huge teams of people was not, after all, where he wanted to be. He felt happy with his decision, and decided to move on, leaving the company a short time after to set up his own small business and work independently.

You may discover that you're getting *no* benefits from your state of inactivity. This is the point where you need to create your very own positive by-products.

For example, a colleague of mine is having great difficulty in giving up smoking despite desperately wanting to quit. A big part of her enjoyment of smoking is that it gives her a sense of belonging – the smokers regularly congregate outside the building and exchange news and gossip. Unless this need is achievable in another way, she's constantly going to be tempted to smoke, not just for the nicotine but also for the sense of belonging that goes with the habit.

When you recognise that your positive by-product is *not* beneficial, leap into action. You may need to stimulate your motivation by redefining your goal, making it more attractive and achievable.

To take some action is far better than doing nothing at all. Sitting on the fence (unless that is where you want to be!) gets you nowhere.

Part IV
Using Motivation in Different Areas of Your Life

'In there somewhere is an ambitious young
man who wants to pass his exams.'

In this part. . .

Now you focus on the key areas of your life, your relationship with those at home and in the workplace, your career, and you even explore how motivation can improve your health and finances. You also discover what helps you develop and grow using some great motivational principles.

Chapter 11

Motivation at Work

*I*f you're lucky you can spend 40 years or more in paid employment – although not always in the same job! Keeping yourself motivated to get up and face another day at your place of work can be challenging. In this chapter, I give you ideas on how to keep yourself motivated throughout your career and working life. I highlight areas where you can improve your motivation, but I also suggest when enough is enough and not pushing yourself too far.

Inspiring Yourself Through Motivation

How far are you along your career path? If you're in your 20s it's likely you are starting out on an exciting new career. If you're in your 30s or 40s you may already have made a number of career moves or changes. If you're in your 50s or 60s you probably have had the experience of working in a variety of jobs and professions during your career.

Take yours truly. I started off in nursing, midwifery, and health visiting. I spent some time overseas before joining a major health care organisation back in the UK. Switching from nursing to sales and business management meant acquiring new and different skills and a vastly different approach to keeping myself motivated to give of my best.

Studying while working full-time also brings challenges, making demands on your family and friends, as well as on yourself. Acquiring new skills and keeping up to date with new methods and technologies involves hard work and effort. What is important is being inspired to keep yourself motivated, keeping in mind that each new skill or qualification you notch up is going to pay dividends in the long run.

Realising what's in it for me

What you're getting out of your job is just as important as what you're putting in. Asking yourself what's in it for me is a good way of checking how motivated you're feeling. If you can't find a benefit in what you're doing, have the courage to stop or change direction, or at least take the opportunity to discuss your concerns with other people.

Maintaining your motivation can be challenging in a number of ways. If you experience several career changes in different companies, what motivates you in one company could be different in another. This can be based on what stage of your life you're at and your own priorities – for example, saving for a house, a trip away, or wanting to gain more experience.

Each job and profession presents different challenges. When I moved from nursing to management I had to rethink how I was going to keep myself motivated as I trod my new career path.

Viewing situations vacant in a new light

Take a look at some of the ways you can maintain your motivation as you follow your career path.

- **Studying and gaining new skills:** Acquiring new or enhancing existing skills and gaining qualifications is an excellent way of maintaining your motivation for the job and propelling you forward on your chosen path. All those long hours of study can also bring financial rewards as well as the feeling of satisfaction and self-worth that comes from successfully completing a course.

  I was speaking to some MBA students recently and they all said that planning their time was the hardest challenge of all. However, they kept up their motivation by telling themselves that the end of their course was only a few months away and the reward was a coveted MBA. To get their course work done they had to make sacrifices, spending less time socialising, exercising, and having hardly any time for drinking! Most of the students said how supportive their families were, motivating them onwards to achieve their goal.

- **Applying for promotion:** Moving up the career ladder and gaining a new position within or outside your organisation or profession means going through interviews, assessments, or even psychometric testing. You need to brush up your interview skills and do research to get all the facts about the new job at your fingertips to prepare yourself for the process. The prospect of a new position, salary increase, and the opportunity to work in a new and exciting area can be great motivating factors.

- **Changing to a new company:** Leaving the comfort zone of a job you know well and moving to a new post can be difficult and challenging.

You need to weigh up the advantages and disadvantages of moving on. Ask yourself what are the factors motivating you to change and whether they are strong enough to carry you through the initial upheaval. You also need to have a firm belief in your self-worth and that your career is going to benefit in the long term from the change.

✔ **Having a change forced on you:** You may find yourself in the position of having to change your job because of redundancy or restructuring in your organisation. Your motivation may be at a low ebb during the process. However, viewing your situation as a time for new opportunities rather than a setback can help to keep you motivated while you are exploring new avenues and job possibilities.

Keep reminding yourself of the potential benefits changing your job or moving to another company brings. The thought that you may regret not grabbing new opportunities falling across your path can, in itself, motivate you into action. It is far better to take a risk and suffer some initial upheaval than to feel that you missed a great opportunity.

Finding out what motivates employees

A UK company called Illumine Training Ltd (see Appendix for more details) specialises in running training courses on a variety of subjects including well-being and motivation. Illumine carried out a survey into what motivates or stops people taking action. Here are some of the respondents' replies, showing what motivates them:

✔ I remember and experience in my mind the feeling I will get when a task is finished.

✔ I need regular encouragement, someone else doing it with me, and someone to be accountable to.

✔ I need encouragement, approval, or support from a tutor, family, and friends.

Deciding to leave your comfort zone

Ben, a student on one of my courses, had a job with a major TV company working in marketing and product design. When I saw him he had been headhunted by a start-up business in the same field. He was very unsure what to do.

As he was talking about the pros and cons of each option, it was fascinating to see how his motivation for the job fluctuated. He realised he was bored in his current position because it lacked challenge and, even though being involved in a start-up business was risky, it was also an exciting prospect. After considering all possible alternatives and realising that working for the start-up company was likely to keep him highly motivated he decided to take the leap of faith and join the new company.

✔ I am motivated by the end result, the feeling of knowing I've completed a challenge.

✔ I need a detailed plan, and a thirst for knowledge and approval and support from my tutor keeps me on track.

✔ I feel excited and challenged by the new role, being able to learn new skills while developing current ones.

✔ I believe that in the middle of difficulty lies opportunity.

✔ I believe that by discovering the passion, you discover the motivation.

✔ I have a clear goal and trust my abilities. I also establish some sort of limit to what I'm trying to achieve.

✔ I visualise what I want, imagine having it, and how that feels. I then take action.

✔ I'm good to myself along the way, giving myself credit for my achievements. For example, I always motivate myself for exams by promising myself a treat once I've passed them. Last year, I bought the car before sitting my exam as I needed just a bit more motivation. I then promised myself I would take it back if I failed! I knew that would *never* happen – it wasn't an option! I ended up getting a distinction!

✔ I break a big task down into smaller, achievable chunks and that makes anything possible, as does telling others about what I'm planning because their enquiries spur me on to doing something about it.

✔ I just find it easier to divide a task into bitesize chunks. They say that if you have to eat a baby elephant, you'd better tackle it in small bits and start sooner rather than later (before it becomes a big jumbo!).

✔ I begin with the end in mind. The clearer the end game and the better able I am to describe the benefits, the more likely I am to make it happen.

✔ My old headmaster used to throw Mars bars at people in assembly when they answered a question well. . .he never missed and we all wanted a Mars bar!

The survey also lists other motivating factors that participants felt were important:

✔ Feeling excited and challenged by a new role. I am able to learn new skills while developing current ones.

✔ Applying for promotion and getting the opportunity to make a difference at a more senior level. I am able to bring about change to a point. However, I am not privy to all the meetings and emails so don't get the opportunity to have an influence in areas where I might if I was at the next level up.

✔ Choosing a new job because of the desire to do something different and giving it a try. I am not afraid of failing. I know that if I went for a change

I would put my all into it and if I wasn't selected it just wasn't meant to be, but I had tried and I would never regret trying.

✔ Working hard for my exams to give me a feeling of achievement and the satisfaction of achieving something on my own. I know that I will improve my own personal development and employability.

✔ Deciding to join a new company as I was unhappy in my old job and knew that only I could control my own destiny.

✔ Wanting to have my skills and knowledge recognised and acknowledged propelled me into changing my job. I also embarked on learning new skills and knowledge to help towards further promotion.

✔ Passing my exams gave me qualifications and the promise of more professional respect, promotion, and more money.

✔ Working to turn around a local charity gave me a personal desire to do a good job. I enjoyed the attention to detail and trusted my own abilities to know what was right to do.

✔ Taking a professional qualification gave me the enjoyment of working with fellow students. I was motivated by the good feedback and support from my tutors.

✔ Studying hard for exams improved my personal development. I gained new knowledge from my studies and increased my chances of a salary rise and future promotion. I was motivated through receiving encouragement from my tutors, family, and friends.

✔ Finding the right vehicle and idea to begin a business gave me the motivation to choose to start and run my own business.

✔ Learning how to fly an aeroplane was motivating for me. I had an understanding flying instructor, who I got on with, as well as the time and money to do it.

✔ Adopting a healthier lifestyle means I am able to enjoy time with my family and have the energy to keep up with the children.

Think about which of these tips can help you get motivated and start putting them into action right away. Survey respondents also identified factors that stop them from taking action, and you can see these in the 'Identifying team barriers' section, later on in this chapter.

Keeping on track

Maintaining your motivation and keeping on track, especially if the going gets tough, means adopting strategies for survival. The following tips can help you:

✔ Having supportive friends around that you can call on for help

✔ Keeping an alternative plan at the ready, giving you other options

✔ Setting realistic deadlines – very tight deadlines can cause panic and be demotivating

✔ Keeping the satisfaction about achieving your goal or task uppermost in your mind, especially if you are feeling low

✔ Getting friends and colleagues regularly to check your progress – so that you always have something to report back

✔ Using a detailed plan of your goal and sticking to it

✔ Building in a reward for when you are feeling low in energy

✔ Asking colleagues for advice if you are facing a difficult challenge. One of your colleagues may have specific expertise in your subject area

✔ If you are struggling to come up with ideas, take yourself off to a place that inspires you. Visit an art gallery or a museum, see a show, or listen to an inspiring and motivational speaker to stimulate new ideas

✔ Reading quotations or stories about people who have struggled against the odds and succeeded: to keep yourself focused instead of giving up easily and dropping out

✔ Making sure that your computer is powerful enough for the job in hand and that you routinely backup files and keep copies

✔ Reminding yourself of your successes: if you're feeling demotivated, telling yourself how good you are can help you get back on course

✔ Being prepared to take risks: failure and bouncing back are part of the learning curve and can be motivating! You learn by your mistakes, giving you the chance to try a different approach or change direction

✔ Believing in yourself: having confidence and self-belief is key to getting on with what you want to do and keeping your motivation going

Using multiple intelligences to strengthen your motivation

Back in the 1980s Professor Howard Gardner came up with the theory of multiple intelligences. He proposed that intelligence is not a single entity but has a number of aspects that he calls the *Seven Intelligences*. Professor Gardner claims that there is more than one way of picking up information, and using the information to bring about change and strengthen motivation. Here are the Seven Intelligences:

✔ **Linguistic:** Reading to get new information or learning a language to boost your linguistic intelligence.

- **Logical-Mathematical:** Prioritising your work to keep you motivated and help you approach tasks logically rather than just doing just what you feel like doing.

- **Musical:** Listening to uplifting music to help concentration, studying, memory, and brain function (such as classical music used in The Mozart Effect). Also by listening to the tone and pace of people's voices or learning to play a musical instrument.

- **Visual-Spatial:** Thinking about the space you are working in, is it stimulating and motivating, or how can you improve your space?

- **Bodily-Kinaesthetic:** Thinking about your posture, how you move and walk. Do you appear as if you are motivated while you are working? Taking up dancing, sport, or other exercise: Pilates can help you gain strength and suppleness.

- **Interpersonal:** Talking to and interacting with people: Neuro-linguistic Programming can be a useful tool for finding out how to interact with people. (Go to Chapter 10 for using NLP as a motivating tool.)

- **Intrapersonal:** Covers the knowledge you have built up from reading, studying, attending lectures or seminars.

Gardner believes individuals have many sides to them. Rather than placing all the emphasis on the first two major intelligences (linguistic and logical-mathematical), he suggests using as many of the Seven Intelligences as you can. Developing your intelligence in other ways can give you a broader view on life and open up new opportunities. Your intelligence can also help you discover links and associations which, in turn, strengthen your understanding, knowledge, and interests, which has a positive impact on your motivation.

Applying any of the Seven Intelligences is likely to boost your motivation to tackle something that before you had little motivation to get started on. You need to choose which of the Seven Intelligences is suitable for the task in hand and think about which is going to be most beneficial. For example, playing creative games (interpersonal) or varying your daily routine (logical-mathematical).

The reward of chocolate!

A friend of mine when she was at university hated writing essays until she discovered chocolate. She promised herself one square of chocolate for every 100 words she wrote. She said it worked a treat! She tried repeating this tactic with her next assignment, but then her willpower let her down. She ate the whole bar of chocolate long before finishing writing the planned number of words! Her strategy for keeping herself motivated just melted away!

A colleague described herself as being intrapersonal. She is very motivated to study, read, and gain new information. Being highly motivated is easier for some people than others. What's important is using as many of the Seven Intelligences as possible to stimulate your motivation, learning, and enjoyment of what you're doing.

Knowing When to Stop

Finding yourself battling away on a task and not getting anywhere, however much you are trying to motivate yourself, is the time to stop and change direction. Pausing and thinking about where you are on your task or in your career, and concentrating on what to do next is your best move. Sitting gazing at the computer screen waiting for inspiration isn't going to solve your problem!

At this stage you may be experiencing a lot of negative thoughts, for example, 'I don't know how to do this', 'What's the point?', 'Why should I bother?' (Now may be a good time for applying the three changes technique described in Chapter 15.) Also rethinking the scope and limiting the boundaries of your task can help you to regain some of your motivation.

Simply giving your mind a rest and doing something different helps. Taking a walk, gardening, or meeting up with a friend can give you the space to reflect on how, when, and if you want to tackle the task again.

A story of determination and numbers

Gary was following a 48-week treatment for Hepatitis C on a combined therapy (1 weekly injection and 6 tablets a day). Unfortunately he had all the expected side effects, people normally only get a few, but Gary had the lot. He even managed to trigger a skin disease that only 1 in 10,000 get. The course of treatment also meant giving up alcohol if the treatment was to succeed. Gary did some positive thinking. Instead of saying to himself I've done 28, 29, 30. . . weeks, he said to himself: x number of injections left to do, x number of weeks/months/

days to go, x number of weeks until I can go back to doing the things I used to do before.

The numbers kept going down, and down. . . till he reached the end of his treatment. He then spent six months convalescing. His method of getting through the course of treatment put him in a positive frame of mind and helped him forget how bad he was feeling. After finishing his 48 weeks, his mum said 'At last, I can use the salad drawer in the fridge again. You won't have any more of those injections to store. I can put food back in there now!'

Prioritising other tasks

Having other pressing tasks distracting you from the project in hand can be the reason why you're experiencing a block. Prioritising and working out a plan helps to get you back on track.

Choose an easy task first, like returning a phone call, taking the dog for a walk, or tidying your desk. Then set about prioritising what you really must do today. Is there anything that you can delegate or keep for another day? Structuring your day can help you to rebuild your motivation.

Rewarding quick wins

Getting a few tasks done immediately can help you feel you are achieving something. You can find it very rewarding ticking jobs off a 'to do' list, even if the jobs are simple, like making a phone call, paying a bill, filing a document. Some people even add items to their to do list after they've completed them simply for the satisfaction of checking them off! Knowing that a job is completely finished can be very positive. Then you can reward yourself with a tea break, lunch break, or walk in the garden. (For much more on rewards refer to Chapter 8.)

A good idea is to reflect at the end of each day on everything you have achieved, however small. Doing this makes you feel good and leaves you in a positive state of mind.

Boosting Your Team

Keeping your team motivated and understanding what makes them tick is important for maintaining morale, efficiency, and productivity.

Organisations use many different techniques for motivating their employees. Every year in the UK a competition is held in *The Sunday Times* to find the best 100 small companies to work for. Each company in the competition gains points based on how they look after their staff in categories including leadership, wellbeing, feelings towards the company, managers, and team members, and opportunities for personal growth. If a company scores the right number of points, the company joins a league table of the 'Best 100 Companies' to work for.

The following list shows the many approaches used by companies to boost morale and motivate their employees. You can try some of the ideas on members of your own team:

- ✔ Publicly recognising small and daily achievements lifts staff morale and often produces better results than offering cash incentives.
- ✔ Remembering to give a personal thank you when a task has been completed. This is especially helpful to staff who are motivated extrinsically. (To find out about being motivated extrinsically go to Chapter 8.)
- ✔ Being an inspirational leader strongly believing in and spreading the word about the company ethos: spending time with your staff and getting to know what is going on in their professional and personal lives (within reason) can also inspire commitment and loyalty.
- ✔ Job-swapping opportunities for short or long periods help staff to understand and appreciate each other's responsibilities.
- ✔ Creating an atmosphere of fun, energy, and excitement throughout the company by organising evening, day, or even weekend outings for staff to get to know one another better.
- ✔ Empowering staff by letting them take responsibility for a project and allowing them the chance of taking risks, being creative, and even making mistakes.
- ✔ Giving rewards such as a £200 gift voucher at a high-class department store, or a haircut by a celebrity stylist.
- ✔ Creating an 'Employee of the Year' award, with a cash prize or winning extra days' holiday.
- ✔ Taking the team out to lunch for achieving targets, letting staff finish early on Fridays, and having a birthday lie-in.
- ✔ Offering a paid sabbatical after 5 or 10 years of service. This can be linked to working with a charity the company supports and, for example, working in Africa for a few months.
- ✔ Encouraging different members of staff to chair meetings each month.
- ✔ Having a family fun day at a theme park for all members of staff to help break down staff barriers.
- ✔ Giving staff the opportunity to work from home, job sharing, and having flexible working practices in place.
- ✔ Keeping staff informed: emailing weekly company updates, having twice-yearly staff briefings, team meetings, and company newsletters.
- ✔ Setting realistic deadlines for projects.
- ✔ Openly praising staff and showing appreciation for jobs well done.

- ✔ Promoting healthy eating by offering a staff 'feel good' fridge stocked with fruit, smoothies, and wholesome cereals.

- ✔ Giving financial assistance and time off for further training, and studying for NVQs or other professional qualifications.

- ✔ Encouraging people to cycle to work by providing secure bicycle parking.

- ✔ Subsidising childcare costs, wellness programmes, gym membership, health insurance schemes, and meeting the legal requirements for maternity and paternity leave.

- ✔ Putting in place regular staff training programmes and team-building events.

Using human desire to motivate your team

Focusing on identifying what is demotivating someone can be used as a tool for tapping into a person's natural human desire to perform at a high level of motivation and productivity.

The human desires include a desire for activity, ownership, power, affiliation, competence, achievement, recognition, and meaning. Making changes within the organisation and cutting out the demotivators can help boost motivation in employees.

All of the following tap into your employees' desire for wanting to give of their best:

- ✔ Building variety into routine tasks to make them more enjoyable

- ✔ Giving employees a say in how they do their work

- ✔ Encouraging responsibility and providing opportunities for promotion

- ✔ Promoting goodwill and teamwork between employees

- ✔ Tolerating errors by avoiding harsh criticism

- ✔ Having ownership of a project

- ✔ Developing goals and challenges for all levels of employees

- ✔ Showing appreciation of work well done

- ✔ Using performance indicators

- ✔ Carrying out performance appraisals

Training your team

Pauline, a former colleague, told me that she had a new manager and was feeling much happier in her job than previously. She said her new manager always had a positive attitude and encouraged the team to actively learn new skills. The team had recently been on a number of short training courses: De Bono's Six Thinking Hats involving creative and lateral thinking, Six Sigma Thinking, Systems Thinking, and Myers–Briggs personality profiling.

Pauline feels the team gets on a lot better after taking part in the courses, which helps them when they are working on projects together. Even though each member of the team has a very different style and personality, she now understands their individual approach to tackling projects.

As well, every month a team member is invited to make a brief presentation on a subject that interests them. Pauline is busy preparing a short talk on Neuro-linguistic Programming to share with her team members.

Pauline is enjoying her job, feels motivated and stimulated, and gets on well with the rest of the team. She is allowed to make decisions and knows that she can approach her manager if she has any queries or questions.

Exploring team goals

Good communication is vital for maintaining motivation and achieving goals. Making sure you have tried and tested communication strategies in place at all levels of the organisation is important. Keeping communication channels open increases the chances of a manager knowing individual and team preferences and being able to respond accordingly.

Communication is a two-way process: managers should talk to employees and vice versa, giving employees and managers the opportunity to discuss their concerns. Keeping all members of the team involved is important in planning and setting team goals, so that all team members are happily working towards the same company objective.

Identifying team barriers

As well as creating a motivating working environment you also need to consider if any barriers exist to your team achieving organisational goals. Some of the following situations were highlighted by a survey asking people what stops them taking action. Do any of these exist in your organisation?

✔ Lack of clear leadership. You can improve this through better communication.

✔ A long hours culture where employees feel they have to work late. You can improve this situation by the boss making a positive first step to leave on time.

✔ No clear channels of communication. Regular team meetings are a good way to tackle this problem.

✔ Impossible deadlines creating undue pressure for employees. Look at revising work priorities to deal with this problem.

✔ A strict hierarchy in place, making it difficult for employees to use their initiative and make their own decisions. You can improve this situation by changing the structure of the organisation or team.

✔ Personality clashes among team members or disruptive team members. 'Away days' for team building can be an effective way of resolving these issues.

✔ Team members demoralising other members of the team with their negativity. You can tackle this by moving the person to another project.

✔ Employees not feeling appreciated. Taking the time to say thank you can help to remedy this situation.

✔ Applying rigid rules and restrictions, stifling creativity. You can improve this situation by introducing more brain storming and creativity sessions.

✔ Team lacking a sense of purpose or direction. Stronger leadership can improve this situation.

✔ No opportunities for team building. A weekly staff lunch, for example, can improve this situation.

✔ A feeling of stagnation among members of the team and not learning anything new. You can tackle this issue by providing opportunities for training.

✔ Other things getting in the way. Reprioritising tasks can improve this situation.

✔ The vastness of a project. You can deal with this by breaking down the task into manageable chunks.

✔ Financial barriers such as fear of investing and losing everything. Good financial advice helps to deal with these barriers.

✔ Lack of time and too many tasks to do. Look at working out what is really important to fit the essentials into the time you have.

✔ Lack of self-belief. You can improve your self-belief by understanding your personal strengths.

Barriers stop people working to their full potential. Often staff turnover and absence rates increase and there can be a general drop in productivity or work performance. Poor morale can affect the whole team, pass to other teams, and affect how people feel about their job and their company. If you discover a barrier you need to act promptly and swiftly, making positive changes and motivating staff to reach their full potential.

ANECDOTE

A teacher's dilemma

A teacher friend was feeling very demotivated. Her husband wrote a poem, which, although, unlikely to win any literary awards, gave them both a laugh and helped my friend feel more in control during what she described as the current upheavals at work.

My headteacher's a silly cold cow, when we need time she wants everything now

She believes in all work and no play, except for her working hours spent on ebay!

On how to manage others she is always unclear, her use of motivation is only fear

She's from the school of 'do as I say', when everyone else sees that's not the way!

Her best skill is putting others down, but they can see it's her who's the clown

Uttering 'well done' is more than she can take, to her it's the way a chef cooks steak!

The head is a bully, who thinks she's always right, she lacks social skills and is not very bright

The moral of *A teacher's dilemma*? Be a motivator – never a terminator!

Chapter 12

Money Matters – Yes and No

In This Chapter

▶ Defining how money motivates you

▶ Sustaining the motivation long term

*I*n the Western world you often sense a feeling that the acquisition of money is a good thing and that enough is never enough. Not everyone lives by this idea, though. Some people are much more motivated by money than others. Everything they do is geared toward getting more money, and they may pass this preference onto their children. Other people are motivated by the things that money can do for them, and some people aren't motivated by money at all. People's attitudes towards money don't seem to be dependent on the amount of money someone has to start with. Spending your early years in poverty can be a lifelong motivator to go on acquiring money, or you could go on living quite happily on a relatively low income.

What part does money play in your life? Does the thought of earning loads of lolly drive you forward or is money just a useful by-product of your job? In this chapter, you take a look at the importance of money and the effect that money can have on your motivation. For some of you money can be a long-term goal while for others it's just a short-term solution.

The Motivating Effects of Money

When did you last receive a financial bonus? Your answer may be recently, several years ago, or not at all. If you've ever received a financial bonus, ask yourself the following questions:

✔ How did I feel?

✔ Did the thought of the bonus inspire me to work harder to make sure of reaching the target date?

✔ Did the bonus make me more positive towards the organisation or persons giving me the reward?

✔ Is money going to influence my motivation in achieving future goals?

The prospect of a financial reward can have a significant impact on someone's motivation to work hard. The financial reward can be for completing a task, reaching a target, winning a competition, or getting a promotion.

For others, money isn't the reason for working hard in their jobs and achieving goals. The job itself drives the person forward. While someone may not turn down a financial offer, money isn't the main motivating factor.

The following stories illustrate the part money can play in the world of work and in daily life.

- ✔ Nick was once a director of a manufacturing company. He was passionate about his work, finding it challenging but very satisfying. He received an excellent financial package which helped pay for his children's education. When he got his annual bonus he decided to treat his family and had a hot tub installed in the garden. After a time though Nick began to feel that a high salary wasn't everything, and the long hours he put in at work were becoming a burden and keeping him away from having fun and time with his young family. Nick found that the incentive of big money was no longer keeping him motivated in his job, his family were far more important, and he eventually stepped down from his role as director in the company.

- ✔ Krystina took the plunge and became self-employed. In the first few years of setting up her business as a consultant and project manager she took on every possible job that came her way, planning to earn the same income as she did as a full-time employee. She worked long hours, usually well into the evening, and often at weekends as well. After 11 years and having established a thriving business network, Krystina realised that money wasn't motivating her like it used to. She thought through her priorities and now keeps her evenings and weekends free and is much more realistic about which projects she agrees to do. She chooses her clients carefully, determined to maintain her work/life balance. Now she just works a few days a week and although her income has dropped dramatically, she is reaping the benefits of having more time to enjoy other parts of her life.

- ✔ Isobel and Bill both work full time. They are in their late twenties and saving up to buy their first home together. They each made a commitment to take on a part-time evening job to boost their income. They also agreed to go out socialising only once a week, instead of their usual three to four nights a week. They also stopped buying new clothes for six months, all to see how much extra money they could save towards the deposit they needed for a house. For Isobel and Bill the actual amount of money they were saving wasn't a motivating factor. It was the thought of owning their own home that kept them going.

Exploring the hierarchy of personal financial needs

Abraham Maslow's 'hierarchy of needs' is a theory that considers different forces that motivate individuals, and which is very relevant to understanding money as a motivator (refer to Chapter 2 for more about Maslow). Maslow suggests that your initial motivators in life are physiological – in other words, in this case having enough money to feed yourself and your family. When you've met that need, Maslow's theory suggests that money will remain an essential motivator until you can put a roof over your head and live safely, with some security. When you have those in place you can begin to think about things like love, self-esteem, and achieving your potential as possible motivators. Until their basic financial needs are met, most people wouldn't consider spending money on non-essential items.

Buying choices

Nowadays you face endless choices when making purchases. What motivates you to buy one particular item rather than another? And are you, for example, motivated enough to queue for hours in the New Year sales just to get through the door first to get your hands on that amazing bargain?

What you pay for goods is linked to a variety of factors: the amount you can afford, the time you have available, how far you are prepared to travel for a bargain, your income level, family budget constraints, and other financial commitments.

Which of the following bargains motivates you into spending your hard-earned cash?

- ✔ Discount electrical and white goods
- ✔ Buy one get one free
- ✔ Off-peak bargain holidays
- ✔ End-of-season stock clearances
- ✔ Closing down sales
- ✔ New Year sales
- ✔ Cut-price grocery items
- ✔ Charity shops for 'as new' clothing
- ✔ Visiting outlet, 'discount' shopping centres

Understanding your buying choices helps you to know if money motivates you as a spender or as a saver. Are you motivated to save money to give you some capital or financial security or are you motivated to save money so that you can afford the house extension or the car of your dreams? Alternatively, you may be the sort of person who is motivated by the instant gratification that a shopping spree brings. You may not necessarily want or need the purchases, but may be one of those people who are highly motivated by this simple act of buying.

Whilst obtaining a bargain can be fun, make sure you don't spend endless hours of wasted time which you could be using more effectively elsewhere. Decide how you can use the money you save to invest in a new project, a key goal, or for something very important to you.

The motivation of a career dream can encourage you to reassess your family income and expenditure to achieve a goal. Many years ago a colleague overseas decided on a career move and set about achieving his dream of becoming a pilot. He had two young children and his wife didn't go out to work, but he needed to find the money to pay for his training leading to his pilot's licence. While he was retraining the family managed to survive on a very small income, shopping carefully, and buying 'end-of-the-day' food bargains. It was a tough time for them, but they came through. My colleague was highly motivated to achieve his goal and since qualifying has had a very successful career as a pilot. The family's initial struggles were more than worthwhile as well as bringing home to them the real value of money.

Reaping the benefits of money

Having enough money to live on is a blessing: if you struggle financially, day-to-day living can be very challenging. Having a comfortable income means stability and security. Frequently talked about benefits of having enough money cover:

- ✔ Making lifestyle choices
- ✔ Allowing freedom
- ✔ Enjoying new opportunities
- ✔ Having fewer worries and pressures
- ✔ Being able to work shorter hours or go part-time
- ✔ Having time to do voluntary work
- ✔ Paying someone else to tackle your DIY projects
- ✔ Helping family and friends financially
- ✔ Being in a position to make donations to charity

✔ Going on holidays abroad

✔ Being able to give your children a better education

✔ Keeping out of debt

Linking financial incentives with goals

Many companies have a policy of linking financial bonuses to targets: in the sales field especially, using incentives is common practice. To assess how an employee is progressing toward a target and to decide the level of bonus the employee receives, most companies carry out a performance appraisal interview. The appraisal is usually between the manager and the employee and takes place before the end-of-year bonus awards.

Performance appraisals are usually made up of a number of factors adding up to an individual performance score. The score an employee gets is directly linked to the amount of bonus he or she receives. Factors can include

✔ Achieving a sales target

✔ Relationships with colleagues and managers

✔ Punctuality

✔ Amount of sick leave taken

✔ Willingness to help others

✔ Ability to work independently

✔ Degree of support to colleagues

✔ Completing tasks, and performance on key projects

Financial rewards have a much greater impact when they are clearly linked to a performance target or goal. People are often more willing to work extra hard on a project when they know there's a financial bonus at the end.

Some people work really hard for several months to achieve their bonus, but slow down markedly for the rest of the year! To sustain the motivation of employees long term, it is important to build other incentives into the job (for more on incentives and rewards refer to Chapter 8) and to not cap bonus schemes so that employees get a bonus based on a percentage of the sales they've generated.

When I was employed as a salesperson the thought of my annual bonus encouraged me to work hard to achieve my sales target. My bonus was linked to my personal performance and also to the performance of the team. Also, a further percentage was paid if the company achieved its predicted profit

margin. In that way the company encouraged and motivated employees to work hard as individuals, within their team, and for the success of the company.

The greater impact that financial rewards have when linked to a performance target or goal applies just as much to your personal life as to your work life. For example, will you be able to treat yourself to a new outfit if you exercise so many times a month, have a spa day as a reward, or go to a special event? Or, in an economic climate where individuals need to reduce household bills, you may be highly motivated to challenge each insurance renewal you receive to see if you can reduce the premium.

If you're trying to quit smoking, you could link that goal to a financial incentive by putting the money you would've spent on cigarette packets each day into a jar. Seeing the money piling up ready for your big treat works as a great motivator.

Keeping the Motivation Going

Think about what financial steps you can take in your personal life to sustain your motivation. How about:

- ✔ Taking coins out of your purse or wallet every evening and putting them in a jar. You'll see the pile of coins grow, acting as a visual motivator and giving you spending money for your holiday, for example.

- ✔ Starting a regular monthly savings plan so you can see your savings grow over a period of time.

- ✔ Selling your clutter and unwanted goods at a car boot sale. This is doubly motivational as you earn some money and declutter your life at the same time!

Always compare the short-term gain of doing or buying something with the long-term gain. For example, investing in a better future for your children through the best education that money can buy, or paying into a pension scheme to make you secure in your old age.

Giving extra pocket money as a reward for being well-behaved at home and at school or doing regular household chores can be a great incentive for children. Instilling a financial incentive at a young age and helping children link work with earning money gives children the opportunity to manage their own money and gives them a valuable life skill.

After a time you may find that money is no longer a motivating factor in your life. Feeling less motivated by money can be for different reasons.

Using financial incentives to renew your motivation to work hard

One of my colleagues in sales who had been working for the company for over 20 years was in the habit of treating herself every year to a new piece of jewellery from her annual bonus. The piece of jewellery, and the nearby discount jewellery centre, motivated her to work really hard to reach her sales target. If she didn't earn her bonus, she felt she wasn't able to justify or afford her treat! Years later, having bought sufficient jewellery, she is now saving for a holiday property overseas, renewing her motivation to work hard for her bonus.

Take Jack, who discovered that being awarded his bonus meant that his salary level went into a higher tax bracket, thereby cutting the financial benefit of the bonus. Jack still found the bonus a motivating factor but he was disappointed at having to pay extra income tax, so achieving his target became less of an incentive.

When the pressure of work becomes so great that it cancels out the value of your bonus, consider a better work–life balance. Looking for a less-demanding job with a lower salary, going part-time, or working for yourself may well be your answer.

Achieving a regular income flow

Having a full-time job gives you a regular income and financial security. However, you may value the flexibility that working part-time or being self-employed allows. Flexible working can bring many benefits such as more time for family and friends, hobbies, and sports. However, there can be drawbacks. If you're self-employed it is often difficult to predict work and cash flows, especially if you are working in an area where there are seasonal ups and downs.

To maintain a regular workflow and cash flow, and to keep motivated, some people adopt the strategy of having a selection of other small businesses to fall back on. For example, a colleague has set up businesses teaching line dancing, exercise classes, and private tutoring. The extra work helps to make sure there is enough money coming in to meet expenses during the quieter periods of the year.

Taking a chance on the lottery

Some winners of the lottery give up working entirely, while others decide to hang onto their jobs. Winning isn't everything and many recognise that work is an essential part of their life, giving them an identity and sense of purpose. However, there are also the lottery winners who, having given up their job, use their winnings to fulfil a dream running their own business. They are motivated not so much by money but more by having a position of power as well as having a great sense of achievement.

Winning the lottery doesn't always bring happiness. Giving up a job and following a life of pleasure can be disastrous. Lottery winners soon come to realise that life is empty and meaningless without the anchor of work and colleagues. Money and spending just isn't enough to feed and motivate the human spirit in the long term.

Chapter 13

Health and Wellbeing

*I*f you have the good fortune to enjoy good health, you're a very lucky person. The World Health Organisation defines *good health* as a 'state of complete physical, mental and social well-being and not merely the absence of disease or infirmity.' Being healthy is about having freedom from illness and disease, and is one of the most important aspects of your life because it allows you to focus on your life itself and your own personal development. Treasure it far above riches and fame! Enjoying a positive state of wellbeing gives you the energy to get on with life and can play a large part in helping you to achieve your goals.

In this chapter, you explore ways of creating a healthier lifestyle and how to get motivated to make changes. To help you on your health journey, I show you how to avoid illness and disease by delving into the unhealthy habits that can tempt you from time to time and throw you off course.

Avoiding Illness and Disease

Maintaining a healthy lifestyle can help you to avoid illness and disease. A variety of factors contribute to an unhealthy lifestyle: lack of exercise, smoking, alcohol, poor nutrition, and stress.

Bad habits impact on your overall health and contribute to illness and disease. Table 13-1 lists lifestyle factors that are linked to specific health problems.

Table 13-1	Lifestyle Factors and Health
Contributory lifestyle factor	*Health problem*
Too much alcohol	Damages the liver, stomach, and peripheral nervous system (arms and legs)
	Stomach cancer
	Raises blood pressure
Smoking cigarettes, cigars, pipes, and excessive passive smoking	Increases risk of cardiovascular disease
	Irritates the stomach, leading to ulcers or stomach cancer
	Mouth, tongue, throat, and lung cancers
Stress	Headaches, migraines
	Ulcers
	Persistent illness – for example, coughs and colds
Too much sun	Sunburn, heat stroke, or skin cancer
Obesity	High blood pressure, heart conditions, Type 2 diabetes
Lack of exercise	Compromises cardiovascular, musculoskeletal, and respiratory systems
	Mental health and mood changes
	Raises blood pressure
	Joint problems, due to poor bone strength and density
	Reduces efficiency of the heart
Poor posture or lifting techniques	Back problems

Creating a Healthier Lifestyle

When you are in tip top condition you have a zest for life. You have energy, enthusiasm, vitality, strength, and endurance. Think back to when you were at your healthiest and most vital. What positive healthy signs did your body show?

What is your health like today? Do you feel on top of the world or are there changes you can make to get yourself fitter and stronger?

Recovering from an illness can be a wake-up call to altering your lifestyle. Your doctor may well recommend a new regime for you to follow. The fear of becoming ill again can be enough to motivate you to make health changes. Or, you have a friend getting over a serious illness, prompting you to make positive changes to your lifestyle.

Improving your health is all about making small, lasting changes over a period of time. You can start by

✔ Cutting down on fat and sugary foods to reduce your cholesterol level

✔ Stopping smoking and drinking less alcohol

✔ Getting more exercise

✔ Taking time out to relax

Pressures in your life, such as family commitments or heavy work responsibilities, can get in the way of maintaining a healthy lifestyle.

Catching the early warning signs is key to getting you motivated to adopt a healthier lifestyle. You may be finding less time for exercise or sport, but eating and drinking more, or having less time to relax and unwind. Early symptoms may occur, showing that your health is being affected, but you may be too busy to notice the signs. You don't have so much energy as you used to, feel slightly out of breath when running to catch the bus, or you notice you've put on weight. You are having headaches, sleepless nights, or just feeling under par.

Early health warning signs motivate some people to action. A health scare can be all they need to motivate themselves. However, others bury their heads in the sand, are scared and unmotivated, and need help to take action. Health education programmes, or advice from their doctor, can help some people. However, for other people, unlocking the door and changing their behaviour is very difficult.

If you've never experienced a healthy lifestyle, it can seem like an unrealistic dream. Or worse, a healthy lifestyle may not appeal to you at all! Whether you're already healthy, striving to be healthy, or need to be persuaded to make a few health changes, the following sections offer useful tips and ideas on how to achieve healthy living.

Deciding your food priorities

There is plenty of medical evidence showing the importance of eating nutritious foods and maintaining a well-balanced diet to keep you healthy. This includes the Government's advice about eating five portions of fruit and vegetables a day. Doctors and dieticians also recommend an adequate intake of protein (animal or vegetable), reasonable amounts of carbohydrate for energy, and milk and dairy products. Keeping sugar and fat levels to a minimum is important, which means cutting down on sweets, pastries, cakes, and biscuits.

What you eat gives your body the vitamins, minerals, and energy stores it needs for growth and development, to combat illness, and to help your body function.

- ✔ Carbohydrates are the fuel for your body. Examples of healthy carbohydrates are: wholegrain bread and pasta, brown rice or basmati rice, potatoes and sweet potatoes, beans, lentils, most fruit and vegetables, unrefined cereals (oats, muesli). Remember if carbohydrates aren't burned off through exercise and activity they are stored in your body as fat.

- ✔ Proteins provide the building blocks for your body, vital for growth. Examples include: lean meat, fish, pulses, beans, dairy products, eggs.

- ✔ Some fat is essential for body growth and development. Healthy sources of fat are: nuts, seeds, oily fish, olive oil, and dairy products.

- ✔ Vitamins and minerals provide your body with essential nutrients. Aim for a variety of colourful and seasonal fruit and vegetables. Examples include: green leafy vegetables, carrots, peppers, tomatoes, berries, grapes, apples, pears, oranges, bananas.

Check whether you're eating the right foods to keep you healthy or whether you have room for improvement. You may need to find a way of motivating yourself to eat healthier options, and giving up sweets, your favourite pie and chips, or takeaway. Having difficulty fitting into your clothes or friends commenting that you've put on weight can spur you on to changing your diet.

If you love chocolate, substitute your craving with dark chocolate containing 70 per cent plus cocoa solids. You often need less chocolate to eat and it's healthier for you.

The positive by-product of eating junk food is the instant hit of gratification and the speed of (or lack of) preparation. To replace the positive by-products, follow quick and easy recipes that are full of taste.

Combine healthy eating ideas when you're socialising with friends. Enjoy preparing a healthy meal or going out to a restaurant to feed the sensual experience of good food.

Choosing what to eat and drink

Are you snacking during the day on chocolate bars, crisps, and sweets? Try some healthier alternatives: fruit, nuts, raw vegetable crudités (carrots, celery, cucumber), oat biscuits with hummus, guacamole, cottage cheese, energy bars (low sugar variety). Keep the unhealthy snacks for high days and holidays.

Drinking plenty of water, herbal teas, Chinese green tea, decaffeinated coffee, and diluted fruit juices is healthier than drinking large quantities of tea and coffee, beer and alcohol. Although those beverages are acceptable in moderation.

Keep to eating three well-balanced meals a day, unless of course the type of work you do, your health condition, or sport or other activities demands a different pattern of eating. Make sure you eat breakfast, this helps to restore the body's energy and keeps you alert throughout the morning. Wholemeal toast, muesli, cereal, porridge, and fruit are all healthy options. If you're someone who loves a cooked breakfast, just be aware of the fat content. Grill bacon and poach eggs instead of frying them. Scrambled, poached, or boiled eggs on toast, grilled tomatoes, mushrooms, and baked beans are all healthier than a fry up.

Get into the habit of eating fish at least two or three times a week. Oily fish such as sardines, herrings, and salmon contain beneficial Omega-3 oils which help brain function and enhance mental processes. Nuts and seeds, for example pumpkin and sunflower seeds, brazil nuts, walnuts, almonds, and cashew nuts, are important sources of nourishment.

Cooking for yourself

Ready-cooked meals, processed foods, and takeaways are readily available and a boon for people leading busy lifestyles. However, they are often high in fat, sugar, and salt. Your body gets far more goodness from eating fresh produce and home-cooked meals.

You may be a person who loves spending time in the kitchen preparing and cooking meals. If you aren't one of those people, you may need a friend to take you step by step through some simple cookery techniques for producing a healthy meal from fresh ingredients. Browsing through cookery books, or watching cookery programmes on TV can inspire you to get started.

I picked up some valuable cooking techniques in my home economics classes at school, and I'm still happily using those basic techniques today. Those early lessons gave me the confidence to experiment with new ingredients and new recipes.

Get cooking by choosing simple recipes and easily available ingredients. Having a few easy recipes up your sleeve helps to keep you motivated and encourages you to build up your collection of menus and healthy options.

To keep yourself motivated, make cooking an enjoyable activity. For example:

- ✔ Have the TV on in the kitchen while you cook
- ✔ Enjoy a glass of wine while sorting out your ingredients
- ✔ Play music or listen to your favourite radio station
- ✔ Get friends in to help with the cooking

For healthy eating, cook meat low in fat or dishes high in protein such as chicken, fish, or tofu. Accompany the protein with a salad or a variety of fresh seasonal vegetables. If you are vegetarian you may need to bump up your protein intake by cooking, for example, pulses and beans. Consider steaming vegetables rather than boiling, Chinese-style stir-frying and grilling rather than frying, and use as little salt as possible.

Here are a few ideas for quick and easy meals:

- ✔ Sardines or poached eggs on toast
- ✔ Grilled salmon on a bed of spinach
- ✔ Stir-fried chicken or turkey with vegetables and noodles
- ✔ Roast chicken or lamb with seasonal vegetables
- ✔ Lamb chops with potatoes and vegetables
- ✔ Vegetable or seafood paella
- ✔ Pasta with tomato, meat, or vegetable sauce
- ✔ Omelette
- ✔ Vegetable soups and wholemeal bread
- ✔ Hot chicken salad
- ✔ Baked potatoes with tuna, baked beans, or chili con carne

 If you are having a go at cooking your own meals from scratch, start off by cooking for yourself two or three times a week initially, rather than every day. The task then won't seem nearly so daunting and will keep you more motivated. Plan ahead and get in all the ingredients you need for the next couple of meals. Cooking does not have to take hours and hours. There are many very healthy and nutritious meals that take only a short time to prepare.

Quitting smoking

All the medical evidence says that smoking is bad for you, nevertheless sometimes it can be hard to give up. Jack was more lucky. He had smoked five a day for over 35 years. However, what eventually persuaded him to stop was falling ill with a chest infection. He was short of breath and in his own words 'felt horrible'. Realising that he never wanted to feel like that again, he stopped immediately. Ten years on and understanding the importance of a healthy lifestyle Jack knows he never wants to take up smoking again and that he was fortunate that smoking for him had never become an addiction.

For someone who has smoked regularly for many years and wants to give up, doing so takes courage and commitment. Fear of the consequences of a lifetime of smoking may, in itself, propel you into action. But a lot of help is around to assist you in reaching your goal, from support groups, peer pressure, nicotine replacement patches, to hypnosis.

The following organisations can offer information and support to help you quit the habit:

- ✔ **ASH (Action on Smoking and Health):** www.ash.org.uk; Tel: +44 (0) 20 7739 5902.
- ✔ **BHF (British Heart Foundation) Smoking Helpline:** www.bhf.org.uk/ keepingyourhearthealthy/preventing_heartdisease/smoking; Tel: 0800 169 1900.
- ✔ **NHS Free Smoking Helpline:** www.nhs.uk/gosmokefree and www. gosmokefree.co.uk; Tel: 0800 169 0 169.
- ✔ **NHS Direct:** www.nhsdirect.nhs.uk; Tel: 0845 4647.
- ✔ **Nicorette:** www.nicorette.co.uk.
- ✔ **Quitline:** www.quit.org.uk; Tel: 0800 00 22 00.

Consider what motivates you to smoke. Is it the effect of your peer groups, your social network, an addiction to nicotine, stress levels, or something else? Knowing the right issues to address can help you to stay motivated.

Think about what would motivate you to give up smoking. Perhaps a health scare, peer pressure, poor skin, the cost of cigarettes, being ostracised, a lack of locations for smoking, or maybe the reductions in health insurance premiums available for some policies.

Staying sober

Excessive drinking over a long period of time can seriously damage your health and make life difficult for those around you. Initially, alcohol has a relaxation effect, making you less anxious. However, alcohol depresses the central nervous system, reducing the efficiency of your brain, impairing your judgment and physical co-ordination, causing blurred vision, slurred speech, and loss of balance. Drinking too much can cause physical damage, increase your risk of some diseases, and make other diseases worse. Some health conditions associated with excessive alcohol include high blood pressure, certain cancers, damage to the brain, heart failure, inflammation of the stomach and pancreas, hepatitis, and cirrhosis of the liver. Drinking a very large amount at one time can lead to unconsciousness, coma, and even death. Experts have also linked excessive drinking to obesity, muscle disease, skin problems, infertility, and sexual problems.

The campaign to reduce drinking and driving has made a significant contribution over the years in helping people understand the importance of not drinking and driving. Taking a taxi or arranging for someone in the group to keep alcohol free and do the driving is the answer for many people.

Alcohol affects people in different ways. The safe limit for one person may be unsafe for someone else. The medical advice is for women to drink no more than 2 units a day and for men 3 units a day, and to have at least one or two alcohol-free days each week.

Measures of alcohol served at home or in bars are often larger than standard measures, and the percentage alcohol by volume can also differ a great deal.

In standard measures, one unit is equivalent to

- ½ pint beer (250 ml, <4% alcohol by volume)
- 1 small glass of wine (75 mls, <13% alcohol by volume)
- 1 small glass of sherry (50 mls, <20% alcohol by volume)
- Single measure of spirit (25 mls, <40% alcohol by volume)

If you're regularly drinking more than this quantity you are increasing your risk of alcohol-related illnesses, and need to decide what you're prepared to do to change your drinking habits.

To help you in changing your drinking habits consider these tips:

- Think about the people you have around that can help you, such as your friends, your social support.
- Set realistic targets for yourself. Set yourself a limit such as three to four units (for men) or two to three (for women) for any one occasion.
- Try alternating alcoholic drinks with soft drinks during an evening out with friends so you replace your 'usual' drink with one containing no alcohol.
- Try some of the non-alcohol drinks and buy beers and wines with lower alcohol content. Keep a supply of non-alcoholic drinks at home.

✔ Aim for at least two alcohol-free days a week.

✔ Slow down your drinking (in other words, sip your drinks).

✔ Consider other ways to help you relax and try other activities instead of a quick lunchtime drink or evening at the pub.

Help is also on hand with these organisations:

✔ **Alcohol Concern:** www.alcoholconcern.org.uk.

✔ **Alcoholics Anonymous:** www.alcoholics-anonymous.org.uk; Tel: 0845 769 7555.

✔ **Down Your Drink:** www.downyourdrink.org.uk.

Be aware that alcohol problems often cover up depression and alcohol is also a depressant, which affects motivation.

Taking time out to relax and recharge

Taking time out to relax and recharge is important for both mind and body. While your body is resting your mind is able to process information unconsciously to help solve problems and answer questions. Taking time to relax can also help you to feel more motivated as you become calmer and less stressed.

Think of a time when you were under pressure to finish something. Perhaps you were rushing from task to task and very likely making mistakes along the way? The saying 'More haste less speed' is very appropriate. Next time you start to rush around, take a moment to pause and refocus to get your mind and body back on track again.

Try recharging your batteries by:

✔ Listening to your favourite music while driving or travelling on the train

✔ Stopping and having a break after working intensively for a long period

✔ Getting up from your desk to take some exercise around the office or go for a walk outside

✔ Closing your eyes and giving your mind a rest in the middle of writing that big report to keep your creative juices flowing

✔ Taking time to listen to the birds singing, and breathing in the fresh air

✔ Making sure you stop for a light and healthy lunch, or to have a cup of tea or glass of water

✔ Curling up with a good book and making yourself comfortable

✔ Enjoying a relaxing bath or long shower

✔ Using up *all* your holiday allowance and booking a holiday

✔ Finding time to work in your garden

✔ Spending time with friends

✔ Taking time to enjoy your favourite hobby or sport

Knowing why your body needs time to relax

Many people spend their lives rushing from one job to the next, trying to balance the demands of home and work. When too much pressure or stress builds up, the body reaches a point where it has difficulty functioning properly. This can affect both your health and your motivation to get on with necessary tasks. If you find yourself in this state it's time to change the situation.

How I relax

I have a special eye relaxation technique that I use when I am travelling on a train or in a place where it is safe to close my eyes for a few moments.

Close your eyes and imagine your eyes slowly moving around a clock face from 3 o'clock, to 6 o'clock, to 9 o'clock, and to 12 o'clock. At each time of the clock, pause and breathe slowly, picturing the following scenes:

✔ 3 o'clock – your favourite holiday destination

✔ 6 o'clock – you are near water, perhaps swimming in the sea, watching dolphins in the ocean, or gazing at a waterfall or fountain. Imagine the water washing away signs of stress or tension

✔ 9 o'clock – you are strolling in the park with your faithful hound or relaxing in your armchair with your beloved cat curled up on your lap

✔ 12 o'clock – you are out in the countryside amongst trees, fresh air, and green grass. Imagine breathing in the fresh air, seeing the blue sky, hearing bird song, and watching the trees swaying gently in the wind

After journeying in your imagination clockwise through each scene, swivel your eyes round and travel anti-clockwise, thinking of each scene as you go and breathing slowly at each time of the clock face.

This technique helps you to exercise your eye muscles, especially if you spend a lot of time in front of a computer. The slower breathing rate also helps your mind and body relax. The whole exercise only takes about two minutes, giving your body a rest and your mind a well-deserved break. You then feel more motivated to apply yourself to whatever tasks lie ahead.

A personal wheel of life

A colleague who is studying for an MBA and simultaneously setting up his new consultancy business uses the following diagram to show the priorities that keep him motivated to be healthy. He has drawn up his own simple wheel of life, with his key priorities in each section. Each priority is a focus to keep him on track and to maintain a balance between his working and home life:

✔ The pound sign represents achieving a financial return from his work.

✔ The heart shape shows the passion in his life.

✔ The four people remind him of importance of maintaining balance with his working and family life.

✔ The smile represents his personal positive thoughts .

Early warning signs of living under too much pressure include

✔ Making mistakes

✔ Interrupting people

✔ Irritability

✔ Feeling anxious or tearful

✔ Poor concentration or memory loss

✔ Having feelings of low self-esteem or lack of confidence

✔ Not sleeping well

✔ Being tired and lacking energy

Take a moment to think about your current lifestyle, commitments, and priorities. Do you need to find more time for rest and relaxation? What simple changes can you make to bring a little more tranquillity into your life?

Feeling motivated to relax

Rather than waiting for the warning signs – such as insomnia, weight increase, drinking too much, irritability, no time for friends – to occur before you decide to act, consider what will motivate you to bring more balance into your life.

Bringing more balance into your life allows time to recharge your brain, increasing your productivity, efficiency, and thinking skills. You'll be able to see situations from a wider perspective, instead of just grinding away, often being more creative with solutions to problems.

Here are some tips to help motivate you to bring more balance into your life:

✔ Pause during your busy day and take time out to relax, allowing time for reflection to help focus your mind.

✔ Give yourself a few moments to relax, giving your mind and body a break to start your first actions towards your goals.

✔ Remember that balancing your life benefits your health.

✔ Discover the best ways for you to relax. For example, reading, socialising, jogging, swimming, window-shopping, meditating, playing or listening to music. Relaxing is an essential life skill.

✔ Remember how well you feel when you're relaxed on holiday.

✔ Think about how much you enjoy Fridays (because it's the beginning of the weekend to give you some time off).

Taking stock when you become ill or making positive changes after an illness

Thomas was coping with a very responsible and hectic job as a director for a major company. He worked very long hours, rarely taking his full holiday quota, and often taking work home to do in the evenings and weekends. Then he was suddenly taken ill and rushed into hospital with a heart problem. Thomas was very lucky; the medical team were able to treat him promptly before his condition became more critical.

Thomas was off work for several weeks and in that time the shock of what happened made him stop in his tracks and check out his life and his priorities. He realised his health was much more important to him than work. After making a good recovery he went back to work four days a week, and through restructuring the company was able to give other people in his team more responsibility and delegate more of Thomas's tasks and jobs. Thomas set a new example to his colleagues by encouraging them to take their full holiday quota, leaving work on time, and where possible cutting the number of deadlines to reduce the pressure on the employees.

A year later Thomas still works only four days a week, using his day off to practise his new hobby of golf, and spending his weekends enjoying the company of his family and friends.

Thomas is one of the lucky ones. He saw the warning signs and took action. So, take time out to relax, recharge, and refocus, it is important for your health and wellbeing.

Making exercise fun

Do you exercise regularly, or play a sport, or have some other physical activity that keeps you fit and healthy? Or are you a bit of a couch potato? Be honest!

The British Heart Foundation and the Department of Health recommend that you do moderate exercise for at least 30 minutes on at least five days each week to maintain a normal healthy lifestyle. The definition of *moderate exercise* means that you feel warmer, your heart rate increases slightly, and you breathe a little faster. Being able to talk after exercising is a sign that the intensity of the exercise is comfortable and you are not exercising too fast.

You can break the 30 minutes down into 10-minute slots to fit into your lifestyle if that's easier.

To lose weight or become fitter you need to exercise harder and for at least 30 to 60 minutes five times a week, to build up the stamina of your heart and lungs, improve your joint mobility and flexibility, increase your muscle strength, and lose weight.

Exercising gains

Benefits you get from regular exercise include

- Increased energy and stamina
- Improved muscle strength and lung function
- Well-functioning heart and lungs
- Weight control
- Stronger immune system
- Lower blood pressure
- Good cholesterol and blood sugar levels
- Makes you feel and look better
- Increased self-esteem and self-confidence
- Reduced stress and improved ability to relax
- Increased supply of oxygen to the brain, helping to improve brain function

Choosing your exercise options

Choose the sort of exercise you enjoy. This motivates you to keep up the good work. You can exercise alone, with friends and family, or as part of a group or organised activity. A love of nature can motivate you to take a walk or some other gentle form of exercise or, if you prefer, doing more vigorous outdoor exercise.

If taking part in a sport or other exercise, or group activity isn't practical or simply doesn't appeal or motivate you, then just try being more active in your everyday life. Get into the habit of walking to or from the bus or train, parking farther away from your place of work, or doing active chores at home. Even though this form of exercise is simple and not too demanding, there are health benefits.

A friend of mine loves dancing and every week drives a long way to her dancing class. She enjoys the exercise, but what really motivates her to dance is her passion for the dance music. There are certain pieces of music which she feels she just HAS to dance to, even if it means dragging an unwilling and unenthusiastic dancing partner on to the floor!

Simple everyday activities are often the easiest to build into your lifestyle.

Here are some simple exercise options:

- Gardening
- Housework
- Walking to and from the station when commuting

✔ Walking your dog, or a neighbour's dog!

✔ Taking the stairs instead of the lift

✔ Swimming

✔ Dancing

✔ Playing outdoors with your children

✔ Supermarket shopping

✔ Ball and racquet games

Walking is one of the easiest and simplest forms of exercise. It is healthy, cheap, and low risk. If you are someone who spends a lot of time sitting in front of a computer, standing up and walking around greatly helps to keep you awake, alert, and your body active.

Going for it when exercising is difficult to do

Okay, so when it's raining outside, what are you going to do? Walking around your home, up and down the stairs, around your office or shopping centre still gives your body some exercise. Taking just a five-minute break benefits your mind and body, so there's no excuse if you have a lot of work to do. Walking clears your head to focus on the task at hand after taking the exercise. If you still find the excuse of high heels to stop you exercising, then keep an old pair of low shoes by your desk and slip into them for your exercise break. However, those who wear high heels might argue that they exercise their legs, thighs, and buttock muscles more, so give it a go!

If you find that despite wanting to exercise you never get around to it, ask yourself what the positive by-product is that you get from this inactivity (see Chapter 4 for more about positive by-products). When you've identified it you can then take steps to ensure that you incorporate this benefit into your life in another way. If you won't exercise because your favourite television programme is on, record the programme, or better still, find an exercise routine you can do during the programme.

Chapter 14

Developing and Growing Your Emotions and Your Behaviour

In This Chapter

▶ Managing your emotions

▶ Moving onwards and upwards

▶ Welcoming change

*T*alking about your inner feelings can be an emotive subject! In this chapter, you find ways of acknowledging, listening to, and managing your emotions. Finding new ways of expressing what you're feeling makes it easier to respond to challenges and gives you the opportunity for personal growth and development.

Setting Out On Your Emotional Journey

> *'Do not wait, the time will never be just right. Start where you stand and work with whatever tools you may have at your command, and better tools will be found as you go along'.*
>
> —Napoleon Hill

Understanding how you're feeling emotionally in a particular situation and knowing how to manage and control your feelings can help you respond in a positive way. Knowing when and if it's appropriate to show what you're feeling can help you get through difficult situations, overcome obstacles, and keep you feeling positive and motivated in your personal and professional life.

Identifying your feelings

Positive emotions make you feel motivated, happy, and enthusiastic about the tasks you are engaged in and life in general. Showing your positive feelings has an uplifting and motivating effect on those around you.

Negative emotions can be draining, playing havoc with relationships, and stifling your emotional growth. Have you ever been so locked in an emotion that you were unable to see the wood for the trees? Experiencing negative emotions can make it harder to think clearly and be rational as well as blunting your responses. It's important to know how to deal with your negative emotions, put bad experiences behind you, and move forward.

Negative emotions do have a place, however. Acknowledging negative emotions is important, especially if a loved one dies, for example, allowing yourself time to grieve. This can sometimes spur you into action to do something to honour a memory. Often a negative situation or failure acts as the catalyst to move you forward, making you more motivated.

Check out whether you have experienced lately, or seen or heard people around you displaying, any of the common emotions listed in Table 14-1. Can you add more to the list?

Table 14-1	Common Emotional Reactions
Negative	*Positive*
Crying	Laughter
Anger	Pleasure
Miserable	Cheerful
Belligerent	Gracious
Irritated	Patient
Dispirited	Exhilarated
Frustrated	Inspired
Mean	Kind
Sad	Happy
Jealous	Trusting
Aggressive	Calm
Aimless	Enthusiastic
Hard-hearted	Forgiving
Despair	Hope
Disgust	Approval
Anxious	Relaxed
Resentful	Generous

Hijacking emotions

Your thoughts and emotions cause an instantaneous physical and chemical reaction in your body called the *physiology of emotion*. If you experience a negative emotion, the chemical reaction can adversely affect your motivation, performance, and the way you communicate.

What you experience inside you is relayed back to the amygdala within the limbic area of the brain (refer to Chapter 9 for more about the workings of the brain). Based on a past experience of a similar situation your body influences how you interpret the current event; whether you face up to the situation or run away. Your response causes the stress hormones to be released so that your heart beats faster, pumping more oxygen to the brain. Your brain cells aren't able to process the information so effectively, and so misinterpret your situation.

Road rage is an emotion that needs to be kept severely under control, both for your own safety and for other road users. Displaying uncontrolled anger on the highway is both dangerous and negative. Your display of anger can be passed onto other drivers, allowing the situation to get out of hand, for example by cutting up another driver, not allowing them access to the junction, and not obeying the rules of the road. You could pass your anger onto other people, compromising your and their safety.

Revealing the hidden message

Usually there is a hidden message, an underlying cause or factor buried deep in the emotion. Sometimes you can be so caught up in the emotion that you forget to stop and take stock of why you're experiencing the feeling.

You can have preconceived notions of how you think things *should* be done. You've built up your ideal map of our world, which isn't necessarily the same as other people's (refer to Chapter 10 for more on this topic). Your view may not be rational or take into account the other person's point of view.

You have a choice about your emotions and how much or little you show to other people. You may feel extremely annoyed, but voicing your extreme anger and all your reactions isn't always appropriate. It may be more appropriate to keep some of the reactions to yourself.

Next time you observe an emotional reaction in someone ask yourself what the emotion is trying to tell you, or what the person is hoping to achieve by his behaviour. Did the emotional reaction in the person have the desired effect, or do you think what he or she was expressing just made them feel worse?

Asking yourself the following questions can help you to understand your emotions and also help you to find ways of dealing with the situation:

✔ How can I react differently?

✔ What could I have said differently?

✔ How might someone else have managed their emotions?

✔ What other responses could I have made?

✔ Are other people likely to respond in the same way as myself?

For example, if you received an incorrect bill in a restaurant, you could politely ask the waiter to check the bill again for you, or you could get annoyed and angry and ask to see the manager immediately. Both reactions will give you a different emotional feeling, and affect the staff and those around you.

To help you unearth your hidden messages, listen carefully to your answers to allow you to move away from the negative emotion. Listening to your intuition can also be a great help in explaining your reactions to what you're experiencing.

Showing what you're feeling is okay and normal. However, in some situations, such as in an important business meeting, it isn't always appropriate or professional to display your emotions. Deciding what's right and proper can be critical. If you still felt that you were swallowing your emotions by the end of the meeting, it would be worth taking time away from the meeting to gain your composure, and then approach the individual again outside the meeting to discuss the issue. This would be a more appropriate tactic than reacting during the meeting when emotions could take over.

Choosing the right responses

In Table 14-2 you see an approach used in cognitive behavioural psychology (or therapy) showing how the mind responds to situations, resulting in different emotions and behaviours.

Table 14-2	How the Mind Responds to Situations	
Thinking	*Emotions*	*Behaviour*
I can't cope	Anxiety	Difficulty making decisions
I can't do this	Anger, fear	Impatient
		Disorganised
		Poor communication

The situation itself isn't causing your emotions; it's how you're *viewing* the situation. You have choices about how you respond to difficult, stressful, or even challenging situations.

For example, if your reaction to a situation is showing how annoyed you are, you can pass that emotion onto other people by your own behaviour. Alternatively, if you're feeling pleased with yourself, your positive emotion shows in your behaviour, making other people feel good.

Try taking control of your thinking, your emotional responses, and behaviour by asking yourself the following questions:

✔ What am I thinking?

✔ Is my thinking helpful and rational?

✔ Are there more helpful or positive thoughts I can take on board?

Consider this situation. A new employee has been offered the chance to work on a project, which you'd presumed would be yours. Your initial reaction is of annoyance and jealousy. You feel undermined, lack confidence, and feel that you're not doing well enough at work.

Take time to ask yourself if your thinking is helpful and rational and then ask yourself 'what would be a more helpful thought?' You realise that the project will involve weekend and evening work and the new employee will gain valuable experience to help them integrate into the team faster. You also realise you're already busy with several projects and would struggle to find the time to work on the new project as well. You realise that you're well respected at work and that you're doing a good job and in hindsight you're delighted you haven't been given this project.

Finding the control buttons again

To help you get your finger on the control buttons, The Centre for Stress Management uses a model called *The 3 As*: alter, avoid, or accept. This model is designed to help you get control of your feelings and emotions and regain a positive state of mind. For example, you feel frustrated because the timescale of your project is going to have to be dramatically extended because key personnel are suddenly leaving the company, taking their expertise with them.

When a situation occurs causing an emotional reaction, try using the 3 A model and asking yourself the following questions:

✔ Can I *alter* the situation in any way?

✔ Can I *avoid* the situation in the future, or the person who caused my reaction?

✔ Do I need to *accept* that I can't change the situation and that instead I need to change my response to it?

Stopping to go forward

To deal with your emotions, you can also use the powerful STOP technique when you feel overwhelmed, when your emotions are controlling you, or if you face potential conflicts with people. The STOP technique gives you the chance of stopping a situation getting out of hand or being misinterpreted, helping you to resolve the situation. Each letter of the STOP technique refers to a positive action you can take to stop your emotional reactions taking over:

- ✔ **S**tep back from the situation: by physically moving or picturing yourself in your mind stepping back.
- ✔ **T**hink: how can you deal with this situation differently?
- ✔ **O**rganise your thoughts: by giving yourself time to focus your mind before making a quick decision, which you may regret later.
- ✔ **P**roceed: after you've had time to think about your reactions and are sure of how you are going forward.

Seeing the end in sight

You can use the visualisation approach (refer to Chapter 6), picturing in your mind a successful outcome and feeling positive emotions. Imagine what success in this situation is going to look like, feel, or sound like. For example, seeing yourself in a video in which you are looking positive and happy.

You can also take control of your breathing to help you relax as you imagine being in a more positive situation. Controlling your breathing has a positive effect on the workings of your body as well as your mind. (See Chapter 13 for additional breathing and relaxation exercises.)

Leaping Forward

Taking a leap forward into a new situation, leaving your comfort zone or people you know, involves having the courage, confidence, trust, self-belief, and financial means, along with the motivation, to take the leap. When you're faced with making a major decision that can change the course of your life, you may find that different thoughts come into your mind trying to stop you:

- ✔ I'm not interested.
- ✔ It's someone else's responsibility.
- ✔ Do I have to?
- ✔ I'm really too busy.

    ✔ I'll think about it later.

    ✔ It sounds fun, but I'm not sure.

    ✔ I might consider it, one day.

    ✔ A bit risky, but worth a try.

Getting motivated to take that leap forward is all about recognising the positive benefits of moving on. For example, signing up for dance classes to avoid stepping on people's toes when you're next at the company dance, going for cookery lessons to avoid embarrassment when friends come to dinner, or signing up for pet obedience classes to avoid your dog running on the busy road. Alternatively, if you're someone who reacts to 'away from' situations (more about 'away from' situations in Chapter 4), you need to be clear in your mind what you're avoiding when thinking about making a change.

Making Personal Changes

Personal changes can be quite simple changes in your life or major life-changing decisions such as moving house, getting married, changing your job, or starting a family. Look at the following list and ask yourself if any of the circumstances influenced your decision to make a change in your life:

    ✔ Attending a presentation

    ✔ Watching an inspiring TV interview

    ✔ Encouragement from family, friends, and colleagues

    ✔ Role models

    ✔ Redundancy

Being career minded

To progress in his career, Daniel realised he needed a Chartered Institute of Personnel and Development (CIPD) qualification. Gaining a CIPD would give him the necessary skills and experience in the management and development of people. To get himself started and in preparation for the CIPD course, Daniel initially enrolled in a series of short training courses in areas which really interested him and motivated him to keep up his attendance. Seeing the benefit of holding a CIPD qualification kept Daniel working hard and gave him the opportunity to climb up the career ladder.

   ✔ Change in personal circumstances

   ✔ Becoming a parent

   ✔ Financial reasons

   ✔ Caring for an elderly person

   ✔ Illness or injury forcing a change in your career

   ✔ Designing a new product that filled a gap in the market

A friend of mine was going through a divorce and was very concerned about how she was going to cope financially after buying a new house. She was particularly concerned about how she would manage the monthly mortgage commitments. The divorce made her double her efforts and she contacted immediately several potential new clients to try to obtain new work. Only a week after I'd been talking to her she won two new secure and long-term contracts, giving her work three days each week. More work gave her the financial security and the confidence to make the leap forward and go out and buy her very own home. When I met her a month later, her house purchase was going through; she was enjoying the new projects and felt more financially secure to help enjoy her new stage of life.

Musical chords

After retiring from teaching Laura thought she'd like to do something different with her time and decided to learn to play the piano. What motivated her initially was the encouragement she had from her family. She felt she had their approval, which was important to her.

However, she was soon receiving unflattering comments from her family that challenged her motivation. She heard them joking about her playing and felt they were being too critical of her progress. Laura was happy to progress at a slow, steady pace and enjoyed the time she spent practising. But she felt demotivated and pressured by her family, who implied she was improving far too slowly.

To help boost her motivation to continue, Laura started recording some of her practice sessions and lessons. In this way she was able to hear for herself how well she was progressing. She didn't need the encouragement and approval of her family now that she was able to tell from her recordings how well she was doing.

Laura realised that what was motivating her to keep on with her piano lessons was how much she enjoyed learning, and although the comments from her family were valuable, they weren't the most important factor motivating her to continue.

Growing and Developing through New Challenges

Experiencing new challenges can help your personal growth and development. Think of some personal challenges you've already experienced in your life and how the experience affected you. These challenges can include moving house, making a career change, learning to drive, or taking up a new sport like hang gliding.

You may find that new challenges aren't always positive experiences initially. But when you look back you realise the new skill you've acquired or what you've overcome and achieved has given you a different perspective on the events, helping you develop and grow.

Embracing change

Embracing change is about courage and commitment, believing in your instinct, and trusting in your decisions. After you've decided on a change, you need to act straight away. Get moving, so that however small the change, you feel you're doing something, rather than just talking or thinking about it.

For example, enrolling in an evening class, arranging to go to the gym twice a week with a friend, removing cakes and biscuits from the cupboards to help you stop eating sweet foods, and so on are all positive steps to help you take a new direction and embrace change.

Taking a financial perspective

Several friends told me what a challenge the Institute of Chartered Accountants (ICA) exams in England were proving to be. The Institute of Chartered Accountants is the largest and most prestigious professional accountancy body in Europe, and the ICA qualification is highly respected. The ICA offers world-class qualifications and the exams are known to be very tough, with a low first-time pass rate. Studying for the exams is a huge commitment requiring dedication and sheer hard work. It's not uncommon for individuals to resit several times before eventually passing all the exams.

At the time, quite a few of my friends considered giving up. However, many years later, with all their studying behind them, they realised that working for the qualification was an invaluable experience, bringing them financial rewards and making a significant change to their career.

Leaving your comfort zone

Leaving your comfort zone can make you feel lost and insecure. But sometimes your hardest decisions are the ones that help you develop and grow the most. The following sections contain some examples of people embracing change and leaving their comfort zone behind.

Going into the unknown Australian outback

Several years ago I had the opportunity as a young 24 year old to go and work in the Australian outback. This meant leaving the familiarity of the modern hospital I was working in, and saying goodbye to all my friends and colleagues. But I knew it was all going to be a wonderful experience and likely change the direction of my future career.

After arriving in Western Australia it took an eight-hour train journey to reach the remote outback area; I had definitely left my comfort zone behind.

Working as a health professional in the Australian outback was a life-changing experience; I felt I had to grow up overnight. I spent a number of years working out there gaining invaluable experience, which has made a positive impact on my life and career.

When the going gets tough, keep going

Juliet instilled in her children from a very early age the family 'rule' that leaving their comfort zone would be good for them. She said that if they ever started something new they had to give it at least three months before even thinking of giving up.

Her daughter still hangs onto this principle and has passed it onto her own children. She realises that it was her sheer persistence that kept her going until she passed her driving test. She also slogged away in her speech and drama classes to gain an Arts Festival Award, even though she wanted to give up many times. Many years later those skills came into their own when she was setting up her nursery for children with disabilities. Her persistence had paid off.

Going it alone

Lisa had been working as a teacher for many years. She loved teaching but decided to fulfil a long-held ambition to set up a teaching consultancy, knowing that she was leaving her comfort zone. To give herself some security Lisa decided to continue working part-time as a teacher while researching and developing her new business.

The services she planned to provide in her teaching consultancy took several months to finalise. Lisa spent time designing a new website and making contacts with schools in different regions where she felt there was a market for her services.

Although Lisa had left her comfort zone she discovered how much she enjoyed acquiring new skills and how motivating it was running her own business. After setting up her new website she found she relished keeping it up to date, checking the statistics, and finding out how many hits she'd received. She felt she had become a website geek! The success of her venture gave her the confidence to give up teaching altogether, embrace change, and become a full-time business-woman.

Chapter 15

Motivating Your Relationships

●●●

In This Chapter

▶ Discovering what motivates your nearest and dearest

▶ Getting to know your colleagues

▶ Taking a look at the individual

▶ Changing your mind

●●●

Sometimes you can be so busy getting on with your life that you have little time left to give much thought to how your words, behaviour, and actions are affecting those people most important to you: family, friends, and colleagues. Enjoying a good relationship with those closest to you and understanding what motivates them can have a positive impact on their lives as well as your own.

Identifying What Motivates Your Family

If you're lucky enough to have family – partner, children, parents, siblings, or close relatives – take a moment to think about how you all get along together. Are you fully aware of what makes your family tick? Do you know what factors motivate or demotivate your nearest and dearest?

You can find that each member of your family interacts with you, and with each other, in different ways. Even where you have strong family ties, what motivates one member of your family can be very different from what motivates the next. Factors such as age, experience of life, and aspirations can give each member of your family their own individual hopes and dreams.

Other factors are also important. Finding out what motivates a person can be picked up from the way he or she thinks and behaves. For example, you see that your daughter is independently minded, preferring to act on her own initiative, making her own decisions, and shunning the limelight (internally referenced), while your son likes hearing praise, being noticed, and going to you for advice (externally referenced). (To find out more on being internally and externally referenced head to Chapter 6.)

Knowing the internal or external likes and dislikes of your family members is a useful start in understanding what factors can impact on their motivation.

Examining your family's motivators

Take a look at the following list to check out which factors can have a positive impact on the key people in your life:

- ✔ Saying a kind word or thank you
- ✔ Giving praise
- ✔ Keeping everyone informed about what's happening in the family
- ✔ Making a timely phone call
- ✔ Offering help with a task or long-term project
- ✔ Being able to spend time listening
- ✔ Sending a thoughtful gift
- ✔ Offering support and encouragement in actions and in words
- ✔ Knowing when to be quiet and leave the person alone
- ✔ Providing advice and a second opinion when appropriate
- ✔ Saying how nice the person is looking today
- ✔ Being enthusiastic

In Table 15-1, list the important people in your life and what motivates each one of them. As you fill in the table, think of specific ways of helping your family members to maintain or enhance their motivation.

Table 15-1	What Motivates My Family
Family member *(List each member)*	*Motivators* *(Give specific examples)*
Example: your elderly aunt	Example: receiving regular phone calls from her children helps her know how they are getting on. She is less inclined to worry about them and is motivated to continue living independently for as long as possible, knowing that help is just a phone call away.

Family member (List each member)	Motivators (Give specific examples)

Meeting your family's preferences

Knowing the likes and dislikes of each member of your family is fine; responding to their needs means making a conscious decision to act. If everyone around you is feeling motivated and happy, it can have a positive impact on everyone in the family.

Meeting the preferences of a family member can be challenging. Individuals often have different ways of approaching and responding to situations, which means that your approach to dealing with a preference can vary from one family member to another. You and the individual need to have mutual respect while at the same time taking into account the effect your actions may have on other family members. (For some useful tips on seeing the other person's point of view refer to Chapter 10.)

Take the example of a family with two or three children. What motivates mum or dad can be quite different from what motivates the children. Each person in the family has different priorities, needs, and ambitions. For the parents the immense pleasure they get from watching their children grow up and develop drives them forward. For the children receiving praise and recognition for their achievements may be a strong motivator for working hard at school. No two families are the same: motivating factors within families are frequently influenced by social, cultural, and religious considerations.

Giving others time to unwind after a busy day

Danny is the chief breadwinner in his family. He enjoys his job, but it is hard work and he feels very tired after his long journey home.

Appreciating how tired he must be when he gets home, Danny's wife makes sure that he has at least 30 minutes to unwind without any distractions from her or the children, allowing him time to change out of his business suit, read the paper, or watch the news on TV. Meanwhile, she keeps the children busy with their homework or other after school activities, stopping the children from pouncing on their father as soon as he walks into the house.

The 30 minutes gives Danny the chance to recharge his batteries, helping him switch from a demanding job to being a full-time father and husband. He is then able to enjoy his family and give his children all the attention they need.

Danny's wife Mary gave up her well-paid job as a finance director to be a full-time wife and mother. Supporting her husband and children and giving them a secure and happy home is her chief motivating factor.

Knowing What Motivates Your Colleagues

You spend a big chunk of your life working, so getting on with your colleagues and knowing what motivates them can be vital to your wellbeing in the workplace.

When joining a company or organisation your colleagues have already been chosen for you. What motivates those working closely with you can impact strongly on your own motivation and how much you enjoy your work.

Take Janene as an example. Janene works as a teacher and is finding the negative attitude of her colleagues draining and demotivating. She feels she is unable to work to her full potential because of constantly being blocked, restricted, or controlled in some way or other by her fellow teachers. Her colleagues' lack of motivation and enthusiasm for the job is contributing to her own dissatisfaction with her role as a teacher.

Creating a motivating support group

Are you about to start on a major project? In an ideal world, you would choose who to have working alongside you. However, you may find yourself in the position of having to involve staff from different departments within the organisation to work on the task. In this situation you may find that individuals bring a variety of skills, different working styles, and preferences to the job in hand. To make sure your project is successful you have to find ways of getting your staff working well together, while at the same time maintaining their motivation to meet the common goal.

If you are able to choose who you work with, you may have the opportunity to choose people you know you get on well with, or have worked effectively with in the past. In this situation the group members can offer support to each other. You're likely to feel happy and motivated working with the group, rather than wasting precious time battling with different egos or personalities. In reality, you will need to work with different groups of people. Taking time to meet with the new group, perhaps over lunch or enjoying a beer or glass of wine after work, can help in breaking down any barriers. Keeping an open mind can also help you to appreciate each person's skills and qualities that they bring to the project, even if their approach is very different from your own.

If you're self-employed and working on your own, taking time to network and meet up with like-minded people can help keep you motivated, provide mutual support, and give you the opportunity of sharing ideas and making new contacts.

Are you putting sufficient time aside to build and develop relationships, getting to know new people, and making time to share thoughts and ideas to keep you and your colleagues motivated and inspired?

Exploring a win/win approach

In business the *win/win* approach has been used for many years to help resolve conflict, and also to achieve happy and successful working relationships. The win/win approach is about making sure that the agenda of both parties is met. Each party has to meet halfway and make concessions to reach a decision agreeable to both sides. Through talking to, listening, and questioning each other you can find out what changes you need to make to bring about an outcome that leaves you both feeling satisfied, positive, and motivated.

Are you a supportive manager?

Being a supportive manager and treating your team well generates goodwill and can pay dividends. Key staff who have been happy working for you often stay in contact after joining a new organisation, even continuing to work on projects with former colleagues and bringing to the attention of their old company new job and business opportunities. Making yourself available to staff at all times inspires feelings of loyalty, encouraging colleagues to speak positively about the organisation long after moving on.

Here are a few tips for bringing about a win/win outcome:

- ✔ Holding on to your self-respect
- ✔ Always respecting the other person
- ✔ Being prepared to express your needs and wishes
- ✔ Allowing the other person to express their needs and wishes
- ✔ Being able to say 'no'
- ✔ Being able to say 'I don't understand' or 'I need help'
- ✔ Having a clear idea of your desired outcome

A technique used in Emotional Intelligence, Neuro-linguistic Programming, and Coaching involves being prepared to make three specific changes when you're trying to resolve conflict or handling a difficult situation:

- ✔ **Changing your thinking:** Consider how you can change your thinking to achieve a more positive outcome.
- ✔ **Changing your circumstances:** Can you change the circumstances in some way? For example, bringing in other people to help resolve the problem.
- ✔ **Changing your physiology:** Sometimes just getting up and moving around or taking a walk can give you the space to get you thinking of other ways of resolving the difficulty.

Acknowledging Individuality

The better you get to know your close colleagues, the better you understand and appreciate their idiosyncrasies, likes and dislikes. For example, Jane, a managing director of a PR company, believes that spending time with her staff is important in maintaining a good working relationship. She holds regular staff review meetings in the relaxed atmosphere of a local café to keep up with what's going on in their professional and personal lives.

Exploring hidden talents

Discovering the hidden talents of people you work with can be rewarding as well as revealing. Being familiar with the hobbies and pastimes of colleagues can give you an insight into what inspires and keeps them motivated. Taking time to look back on past projects, jobs, and travel experiences can help you unearth skills and talents in your colleagues that you didn't know existed. For example, recently I was chatting to a colleague and found out by chance that she had lived in Japan when she was a teenager and is still fluent in Japanese; an asset that I know I can turn to good use in my company.

Embracing personal choice

Encouraging the people you work with to express their individuality and allowing them to follow their personal preferences stimulates positive feelings towards the organisation and boosts motivation.

One company I know has a points scheme as a way of motivating staff, as well as allowing its staff freedom of choice in the prizes they take home. When an employee has gained a certain number of points, he or she can name their prize (within reason!). As the points are earned they are chalked up on the board, giving staff public recognition of their achievements in a spirit of friendly competition.

Tuning into other people's values

You find that mostly everyone you meet has a set of values, often based on age, upbringing, and family influences. If a person holds the same values as yourself, you are immediately on a comfortable footing. However, you need to be aware that other people can hold quite a different set of values to yours. Taking the trouble to discover the values and beliefs of those around you encourages good relationships, making working together a positive and valuable experience.

Photographing your hidden talents

A major computer manufacturer came up with a brilliant idea for getting to know its staff better. The company asked its employees if they would allow it to take photos of each of them engaged in their favourite pastime or hobby. The photos were then displayed as posters all around the company for everyone to view. Finding out what fellow workers did on their day off had a positive impact throughout the company.

Each employee was now seen in a new light. Beneath the business suit lurked a wannabe football or tennis star, or chess champion. The photos showed employees displaying skills and talents hitherto unknown to the company, helping to enhance morale, generate mutual respect, and boost motivation at all levels.

Values can include integrity, loyalty, openness, generosity, respect, fairness, and honesty. If a colleague believes that a task doesn't match his or her values, you need to address the problem and honour their values by finding a more suitable task or rethinking the task in hand. (You can find out more about values in Chapter 4.)

Thinking about individual preferences

Have you ever been in the situation where you were surprised when someone reacted to what you said or did in a totally unexpected way? Or, you overheard someone describing an event that you both witnessed but from the other person's account could well have been an entirely different happening? Be assured, this is normal and is linked to your individuality as well as the way your brain processes information. (Refer to Chapter 9 to find out how your brain works.)

Being aware of individual preferences and seeing alternative approaches to situations is a way of acknowledging individuality and helps to keep those around you motivated.

Discovering Your Mindsets

Taking time to explore your mindsets can help you understand how you react in certain relationships and life situations. A *mindset* is a fixed attitude or a habit of mind that determines how you interpret and respond to situations. Your beliefs and values can be part of your mindset, making how you act a foregone conclusion. For example, holding the firm belief that 'Work is *always* fun' can give you a fixed mindset. Discovering a person's mindset can be the key to understanding their potential and acknowledging their individuality.

Nevertheless, the good news is that mindsets can be changed as you discover new ways of looking at situations as you become better informed. Uncovering mindsets is a tool used in the world of business to find new ways of approaching situations, embracing new ideas, encouraging participation and stimulating motivation, and empowering everyone in the organisation.

You can change your mindset by being open to other views, through talking, listening, and asking questions. What you are fixed on doing can then be adjusted or amended as you gather more information, analyse the facts, and use the data to give you a fresh perspective.

When a new approach to a situation is taken on board, it is important to keep up the momentum by carrying out the agreed changes promptly. However, you should always bear in mind that some people can feel reluctant to or resist changing their mindset. In this situation you should act with tact and consideration, or even leave well alone.

Changing a person's mindset is a two-way process, you need to be willing to change as well. (See 'Exploring a win/win approach' earlier in this chapter.)

Knowing why mindsets matter

Research done over 35 years by Professor Carol Dweck and her colleagues at Columbia and Stanford Universities shows how mindsets can affect motivation and achievement. Carol Dweck's findings emphasise that mindsets can shape your goals, your attitude towards work and relationships, and predict whether you are going to fulfil your potential.

Carol Dweck and her colleagues have come up with two basic mindsets:

- ✔ **Growth (Incremental) Mindset:** This is where a person actively enjoys having opportunities to learn and become more competent at a task, even if their achievement is seen to be less than perfect by others. People holding a Growth Mindset are often confident, robust, and happy to learn from failure.

- ✔ **Fixed (Entity) Mindset:** People believe that they cannot change what they were born with and that they are bound to fail before they start. People with a Fixed Mindset often avoid opportunities to improve their skills and abilities because the effort required won't make any difference, and trying to improve a skill only proves that they weren't good at it in the first place. A person holding a Fixed Mindset usually lacks self-confidence and needs constant praise to achieve.

Carol Dweck's research also shows that it is possible to maintain a Fixed Mindset in one area of your life (for example, believing you are hopeless at sport) and a Growth Mindset in another area (you love learning languages).

You are much more likely to be successful in life if you hold a Growth Mindset. Carol Dweck's research with university students found that Growth Mindset students achieved significantly better grades than Fixed Mindset students, regardless of how they scored in intelligence tests. Intelligence isn't fixed but grows with effort and practice.

Your brain is like a muscle, it improves with healthy exercise – it's never too late to set about modifying your mindset!

Changing your mindset

To understand what's happening when you relate to another person, you can either imagine having a dialogue with yourself or consider what mindset the other person is using.

Try using Carol Dweck's 4-step approach to changing your mindset (used with permission):

1. **Learn to hear your Fixed Mindset voice.**

2. **Recognise that you have a choice.**

3. **Talk back to your Fixed Mindset with a Growth Mindset.**

4. **Switch to the Growth Mindset action.**

The following sections give you practical help in achieving each step.

Step 1: Hearing your Fixed Mindset voice

As you approach a challenge, your Fixed Mindset voice is saying:

- Are you sure you can do it?

- Maybe you don't have the talent.

- What if you don't achieve – you'll be a failure.

- People will laugh at you for thinking you had talent.

- If you don't try, you can protect yourself and keep your dignity.

As you hit a setback, your Fixed Mindset voice is saying:

- This would have been easy if you really had talent.

- You see, I told you it was a risk. Now you've gone and shown the world how limited you are.

- It's not too late to back out, make excuses, and try to regain your dignity.

As you face criticism, from your Fixed Mindset you hear your voice saying:

- It's not my fault. It was something or someone else's fault.

- You are feeling angry at the person who is giving you feedback. 'Who do they think they are? I'll put them in their place.'

- The other person may be giving you specific, constructive feedback, but you are hearing them say 'I'm really disappointed in you. I thought you were capable but now I see you're not.'

Step 2: Recognising that you have a choice

It's your choice how you handle challenges, setbacks, and criticism. Hanging on to your Fixed Mindset is a sign that your talents or abilities are lacking. Or, you can interpret the challenges, setbacks, and criticism as a Growth Mindset, pushing yourself onwards and upwards to achieve your goal. It's up to you.

Step 3: Talking back with a Growth Mindset voice

As you approach a challenge, ask yourself the following questions to help speak to your Fixed or Growth Mindset.

FIXED MINDSET (FM): 'Are you sure you can do it? Maybe you don't have the talent.'

GROWTH MINDSET (GM): 'I'm not sure I can do it now, but I think I can achieve with time and effort.'

FM: 'What if you don't achieve – you'll be a failure.'

GM: 'Most successful people stumble or fail along the way.'

FM: 'If you don't try, you can protect yourself and keep your dignity.'

GM: 'If I don't try, I automatically fail. Where's the dignity in that?'

As you hit a setback:

FM: 'This would have been easy if you really had talent.'

GM: 'That is so wrong. Basketball wasn't easy for Michael Jordan and science wasn't easy for Thomas Edison. They had a passion and put in tons of effort.'

As you face criticism:

FM: 'It's not my fault. It was something or someone else's fault.'

GM: 'If I don't take responsibility, I can't fix it. Let me listen — however painful it is – and learn whatever I can.'

Step 4: Taking the Growth Mindset action

It's your choice which voice you follow: Fixed Mindset or Growth Mindset.

Throw yourself into the challenge, hearing the criticism, learning from your setbacks, and trying again. You hold your next actions in your own hands.

Practise hearing your Fixed Mindset voice and your Growth Mindset voice, then take the Growth Mindset action.

Taking time to explore Fixed and Growth Mindsets can help when relating to other people and acknowledging their individuality.

Part V
The Part of Tens

'You told me to find a famous person whose example would motivate me in the workplace. I did— Tiger Woods!'

In this part. . .

Here I give you some of my favourite tips and ideas for keeping yourself motivated and how to put them into practice. You read about ten amazing and inspirational people, have the chance of doing some great motivational exercises to boost your motivation further, and get to think about some daily actions you can take to keep your motivational levels high.

Chapter 16

Ten Great Motivating People

In This Chapter

▶ Finding motivating role models

▶ Being inspired to get moving

▶ Discovering secrets of motivation

Motivation is the catalyst that gets you leaping into action and moving forward. The ten people in this chapter stand out for being highly motivated and wanting to be best in their field. Take a moment to weigh up what's so special about each person. What is it about them that inspires you? Is it their values, their approach to life, their determination? Hopefully, their stories are going to inspire you and spur you into action.

David Beckham

David Beckham's fame stretches far beyond the football pitch – his name is an international brand. From a working-class background he has risen to stardom through talent and sheer hard work. The boy with the 'golden boot' is an inspiration to aspiring football players not only in Britain but throughout the world. Beckham is idolised by fans and is more photographed than the Queen. When he and his equally famous wife Victoria Beckham bought their 1930s Hertfordshire mansion in 1999, it was quickly dubbed 'Beckingham Palace'.

Beckham, now 33, was born in east London on May 2, 1975. At the age of 17, he joined Manchester United and in the 1996 season was given the 'Number 10' shirt – outlets must have sold more replicas than can possibly be counted. In 2004 Beckham was the world's highest-paid footballer. While playing for Madrid Beckham became the first British football player to play 100 Champions League matches. This was followed up in 2008 by earning his 100th cap for England in a match against France.

At the 'Greatest Britains 2007' awards David Beckham was voted Britain's Greatest Ambassador. Ever since his days at Manchester United Beckham has supported UNICEF and is now a Goodwill Ambassador for the organisation. Amongst his numerous other activities Beckham has set up football academies in many parts of the world to inspire and motivate youngsters to take up the sport. Beckham is truly a legend in his own lifetime and an inspiration to many young people.

In interviews, David says that he is motivated by winning trophies and looking forward to winning the next one. He is also driven by a fear of not letting people down, by helping to raise the profile of sport throughout the world, and by a genuine desire to raise money for charity.

Richard Branson

Sir Richard Branson must be the most famous entrepreneur of all time. He is flamboyant, competitive, and inspirational, and his Virgin brand covers everything from travel and tourism to leisure and pleasure, shopping, media and telecommunications, finance and money, health, social and environmental concerns – and that's just a start! He is now the world's 236th richest person, and uses his wealth for many good causes.

Born in 1950, Richard, while at school and only 16 years old, started up his first charity to help young people, called the 'Student Advisory Centre'. Shortly after leaving school, and although dogged with dyslexia, he set off on his business career and, aged 20, founded the Virgin brand by opening his chain of record stores, Virgin Records, later known as Virgin Megastores and rebranded as Zavvi in late 2007. Virgin Records' first release was Mike Oldfield's *Tubular Bells*, which was a bestseller and British LP chart topper. The Virgin brand grew rapidly during the 1980s – Branson setting up Virgin Atlantic Airways and expanding the Virgin Records music label, to name but two new ventures.

Branson is a transformational leader through his down-to-earth nature, his resilience, his determination to succeed, and his vision for exploring worldwide initiatives as a brand builder. He quotes being unafraid of failure as an important quality of a champion, and sets himself huge challenges fuelled in his earlier years by his grandmother, who, at the age of 99, said 'you've got one go in life, so make the most of it'. He actively encourages innovation, has a strong sense of trust amongst his worldwide team, delegates decision making, and ensures he has time for his family and holidays.

To keep himself motivated and his adrenaline rush high, Branson has been involved in a number of world record-breaking attempts. For example, in 1991 he crossed the Pacific Ocean by balloon from Japan to Canada, a distance of 6,700 miles. Branson lives every minute to the full. In business circles he is seen as a 'transformational leader'. He is continually interested in learning new things, and never stops. As he says, 'A business has to be involving, it has to be fun, and it has to exercise your creative instincts'. Branson describes Virgin as a way of life which he enjoys and says how every day is like the long university education he never had. He has an unfailingly positive approach to life, showing innovation and daring in everything he does. He is driven by effort and opportunity, and enjoys meeting new people every day, challenging them, and being challenged. He understands his limitations, surrounds himself with talented and brilliant people, and believes in having fun.

Winston Churchill

Sir Winston Leonard Spencer-Churchill, (November 30 1874–January 24 1965) became British Prime Minister at the beginning of the Second World War. He was a brilliant statesman, leader, and orator. His greatest achievement was his refusal to give in when defeat seemed imminent – and saying never to negotiating with Germany. His famous and passionate wartime speeches 'I have nothing to offer but blood, toil, tears, and sweat', 'Let us therefore brace ourselves to our duties . . . men will still say, "This is our finest hour"', and 'We shall fight on the beaches . . . we shall never surrender' stirred millions and sent shivers down the spine. Some of his most ardent admirers have even claimed that it was actually Mr Churchill who won the war!

Although born in a palace, life had its difficulties for Churchill, like ordinary people. He was a lonely child, seeing little of his parents and throughout his life worked hard to overcome a speech impediment. It was later said of him that he excelled because of, rather than in spite of, his speech defect. But he was independent and at times rebellious. He was also physically brave, training as a soldier, and fighting alongside fellow men in the Boer War in South Africa, where he was captured, imprisoned in Pretoria, and finally escaped back to Britain.

What drove Churchill was a passion to defeat the enemy, both outside and within, whatever the odds. He was motivated by a love of his country and its people. Thanks to his stirring speeches and his steadfast determination in the face of the enemy, he, in turn, proved to be a source of inspiration and motivation for the British people, and a strong leader during the country's darkest hours.

Lewis Hamilton

Lewis Hamilton, the 23-year-old British Formula One racing driver from Stevenage, Hertfordshire, made an explosive arrival on the F1 scene, making front-page headlines during his stunning 2007 debut season. His success has caught the imagination of the nation. In his first season he thrilled the world of motor racing with his victories in Canada, America, Hungary, and Japan.

His story is as inspiring as it is motivating. He is something of a child prodigy. As a child he was racing remote-controlled cars in competitions and winning against adults. At the tender age of eight little Lewis Hamilton, the youngster from a difficult background, approached McLaren team boss Ron Dennis at an awards ceremony and told Dennis that one day he was going to drive for McLaren. Impressed, Ron Dennis later took Lewis under his wing and at the age of 13 Lewis was signed up for the prestigious McLaren Driver Development Support Programme. Sheer guts, determination, hard work, and confidence made it possible for Hamilton to break through the barriers and enter the rich man's world of motor racing. To crown his achievements, Lewis was voted runner-up in the BBC Sports Personality of the Year 2007, and was also given the Pride of Britain 'Most Inspiring Public Figure' award.

Hamilton describes his motivator as a desire to be the best at whatever he decides to put his mind to. He describes the strength his inner self has to not let him give up unless he's achieved his goal. As an inspiration to others, his key focus is his aim to win, and his belief that he will do whatever it mentally and physically takes to win.

Nelson Mandela

Nelson Rolihlahia Mandela became the first black President of South Africa, leading his country into a new era of freedom and democracy. Born on 18 July, 1918, he trained as a lawyer and joined the African Nationalist Congress (ANC), eventually becoming its leader. Mandela realised that the black people of South Africa must submit to apartheid or fight, and chose a policy of political activism. In 1964 he, along with other ANC activists, was convicted of crimes including sabotage and Mandela spent the next 27 years in prison. From prison, Mandela spearheaded the long struggle against apartheid.

During his trial in 1964, Nelson Mandela made his dignified and memorable speech declaring that non-racial democracy was 'An ideal for which I am prepared to die', a speech that stirred the conscience of the world but left the implacable South African government unmoved.

Although Mandela's father was a member of the Xhosa royal house, the young Mandela lived in poverty. He's often known as Madiba, an honorary title adopted by elders of Mandela's clan, and Rolihlahia can be translated as 'troublemaker'. As a child Mandela was brought up to observe but never ask questions. Later in life he was shocked to visit the homes of white people and hear children firing questions at their parents and expecting answers.

Mandela is motivational in his unique leadership skills and in his amazing achievements when facing adversity with dignity. On his release from prison in 1990 he led the movement for peace and reconciliation in South Africa. He has received more than 100 awards over four decades, most notably the Nobel Peace Prize in 1993. Nelson Mandela's name stands as a symbol of freedom and equality. In 1998 *The Guardian* wrote of him 'Few people in recorded history have been the subject of such high expectations; still fewer have matched them; Mandela has exceeded them'.

Jamie Oliver

Jamie Oliver (born 27 May, 1975), the youthful celebrity chef, is a household name. He first came to fame in the TV series *The Naked Chef*, a reference to the simplicity of his recipes: keep it fresh and natural. Passionate about the benefits of eating fresh, organic foods Jamie stirred the nation into action by his campaign for improving the standard of school meals in British schools in his TV show *Jamie's School Dinners*. Making full use of his celebrity status he lobbied the Government to support his cause, with some success. His success to date has been acknowledged by being named 'Most Inspiring Political Figure of 2005' in the Channel 4 Political Awards, 2006. He also received the prestigious Beacon Fellowship Prize in 2005 for his contribution to disadvantaged young people.

At the age of 33, Jamie Oliver is reported to be worth an estimated £25 million. Wanting to do something positive with his wealth and fame, Jamie set up the 'Fifteen' charity restaurant, where he trained 15 disadvantaged young people to work in the hospitality industry, and following the success of this venture he opened more Fifteens around the globe: Fifteen Amsterdam, Fifteen Cornwall, and Fifteen Melbourne with Australian friend and fellow chef, Tobie Puttock. Getting the original Fifteen up and running was documented in the TV series *Jamie's Kitchen*.

Jamie Oliver is driven by his strongly held belief that eating well is key to the nation's health. He is motivational to others in the way he leads people by focusing on several principles, including communicating a clear vision, setting good examples to his team, and having the attitude to carry the can if things go wrong. If one way of tackling a problem doesn't work, he tries another.

The Queen

Queen Elizabeth II (born 21 April, 1926) is Queen of the United Kingdom and the Commonwealth. The Queen is admired for her natural charm, strong sense of duty, steadfast Christian beliefs, hard work, and longevity. She's currently the second longest-serving head of state in the world. On 21 December, 2007, the Queen outdid her great-great grandmother Queen Victoria as the oldest reigning monarch in British history.

As well as witnessing many changes to the British constitution and big changes in the social and cultural life of Britain, the Queen hasn't been without her share of personal and private sorrows. The Royal Family went through a bad patch in the 1990s when the credibility of the monarchy was damaged by the breakup of the marriages of Charles and Diana, and Andrew and Fergie. A large number of people began to see the monarchy as outdated and serving no particular purpose. But the Queen kept her foothold. In the BBC TV film *A Question of Attribution* the Queen, played by Prunella Scales, is seen as immensely hard working, eager for knowledge, witty, and knowing. And in the recent film *The Queen* starring Helen Mirren and Michael Sheen, Elizabeth II is portrayed sympathetically, a woman struggling between public and private duty in her response to the sudden death of Diana, Princess of Wales. In real life her Golden Jubilee celebrations in 2002 were a huge success; the public celebrations including the first ever pop concert in the gardens of Buckingham Palace.

Shortly before her 80th birthday a poll was carried out showing that the majority of the British public wanted the Queen to stay on the throne until her death – many feeling that she is an institution in herself. Long live the Queen!

JK Rowling

JK Rowling, born on 31 July, 1965, is the author of the hugely popular *Harry Potter* fantasy series and is the most successful writer for children (and not forgetting adults), ever! Her Harry Potter books have gained worldwide attention, won multiple awards, and sold nearly 400 million copies. Harry Potter is now a global brand worth an estimated £7 billion, and the last four Harry Potter books have consecutively set records as the fastest-selling books in history. The Harry Potter output totals 4,195 pages, and has been translated, in whole or in part, into 65 different languages.

The 2007 *Sunday Times Rich List* estimated Rowling's fortune at £545 million, ranking her as the 136th richest person in the world and the 13th richest woman in Britain. Forbes names Rowling the second-richest female entertainer in the world and ranks her as the 48th most powerful celebrity of 2007.

So how did it all happen? The story goes that the inspiration for Harry Potter came to her in 1990 while she was sitting on a train delayed for 4 hours travelling from Manchester to London. Three cheers for the British transport system! After the breakup of her marriage she became a lone parent with a baby daughter to support. She had always had a fertile imagination and had been scribbling stories ever since she was a girl. While her baby daughter slept she took the opportunity to get pen to paper and *Harry Potter and the Philosopher's Stone* was born, sent off to the publisher Bloomsbury, and the rest is history. . .

JK Rowling's greatest achievement is almost certainly that she has caught the imagination of children everywhere with her rich, demanding, and action-packed stories. She has given immense pleasure to millions. A committed Christian, her values and beliefs shine through her books. Added to this she is a notable philanthropist, supporting such charities as Comic Relief, the Multiple Sclerosis Society of Great Britain, and One Parent Families. If you ask JK Rowling's fans what's best about the Harry Potter books, you always get the same reply: 'you simply can't put them down'.

JK Rowling is motivational to others in what she has achieved, in how she has overcome personal struggles to achieve so much, and in her amazing inspiration to so many people throughout the world.

Margaret Thatcher

Baroness Thatcher (born 13 October, 1925) is most famous for being Britain's first ever woman Prime Minister, and for winning three consecutive general elections for the Conservative party. Margaret Thatcher dominated British politics in the last 20 years of the 20th century. She was admired for her tremendous drive, unshakeable political convictions, and was said to need only four hours' sleep a night!

Margaret Thatcher was adored by her followers and loathed by her enemies. There was never room for compromise. Early on in her career in the 1970s when she was Secretary of State for Education and Science she earned herself the title 'Thatcher, Thatcher, Milk Snatcher' when she abolished free school milk for 7 to 11 year olds. And in 1976 as Leader of the Opposition she was dubbed the 'Iron Lady' by the Soviets: a name she took delight in, believing it aptly summed up her character as unwavering and steadfast. When in power, she pursued an unrelenting policy of privatising state-owned industries and utilities, reforming the trade unions, lowering taxes, and reducing social expenditure across the board; policies that succeeded in cutting inflation, but made unemployment soar.

There's no doubt that Margaret Thatcher in office was a remarkable woman. But her divisive politics, particularly her scheme for a Poll Tax, caused her downfall and forced her to resign. When she resigned people were dumbfounded. For many young people she was the only Prime Minister they had *ever known*.

Margaret Thatcher has been inspirational to people in her worldwide influence amongst men and women, with her strong personality and character amongst her strengths. She demonstrated a feeling of commitment, showing class, intelligence, and tremendous effectiveness as a woman in a man's world.

Tiger Woods

'Tiger' Woods was born on 30 December, 1975, in Cypress, California. He is currently the World No. 1 professional golfer and his achievements to date rank him amongst the most successful golfers of all time. Added to this he was the highest-paid professional athlete in the world in 2006. He makes $50 million dollars a year in endorsements and another $5 million playing golf. Surely a record hard to beat!

More inspirational people

Consider the following list of people. You may also find them inspirational to you.

✔ **Professor Stephen Hawkins,** for contributing to outstanding scientific development throughout the world alongside his steadfast determination to fight against his debilitating motor neurone disease.

✔ **Ellen MacArthur,** for overcoming immense challenges as the youngest person and fastest woman to sail around the world alone. An outstanding sailor bringing sailing alive to millions.

✔ **Madonna,** for her belief in moving with the times and never standing still, and having the courage to keep on reinventing herself.

✔ **Sir Steve Redgrave,** for managing his diabetes and not letting it get in the way of competing in the gruelling sport of rowing, and for being an inspirational Olympic champion.

✔ **Anita Roddick,** for founding The Body Shop and for her passion and enthusiasm for producing only natural cosmetics.

✔ **Jane Tomlinson,** for showing phenomenal spirit and strength after being given just months to live. She battled on raising hundreds of thousands of pounds for charity and died, seven years later, aged 43. Jane's mission in life was a simple one: to make the most of every day and to help others. She not only achieved that several times over, but is a true inspiration for millions of people suffering from cancer.

How does he do it? Well, by being good at golf. He was a child prodigy. He first started playing golf when he was 2 years old and doesn't seem to have stopped since. He won the Junior World Championship six times, became a pro in 1996, and has never looked back. He has more career major wins and career PGA Tour wins than any other active golfer. He is the youngest player to achieve the career Grand Slam, and the youngest and fastest to win 50 tournaments on Tour.

But his major achievement is stimulating a huge surge of interest in the game of golf, especially from the multiracial audience who previously viewed golf as white and elitist, and at the same time doubling attendance and TV ratings. Tiger has given as much to the game as he has taken from it.

Tiger is motivated by his sheer love of the sport, golf driving him ever on. By nature Tiger says he is stubborn and impatient but tries to control his feelings by practising Buddhism. He is truly of mixed race, with even a bit of Dutch in him and was given the name Tiger by a Vietnamese soldier friend of his father. He is a role model for aspiring young golfers worldwide. After Tiger turned professional, one sports writer said of his talent 'He's not just a promising Tour pro any more, he's an era'. And a grateful fan declared 'Thanks to the Woods family for giving the entire world something to do at the weekends!'

Chapter 17

Ten (Or So) Motivational Exercises

Motivational exercises are a great way of getting you moving and giving you a new lease of life. This chapter describes ten or so exercises to help you build up your enthusiasm for your task.

Using Similes to Boost Your Motivation

A *simile* is a figure of speech and can help you to think around a challenge in a more creative way. The idea is to find as many associations or links as possible with the challenge.

Take the following examples of similes:

✔ **How is** .... like winning a transatlantic yacht race?

✔ **How is** .... like climbing a mountain?

✔ **How is** .... like cooking a meal for a dinner party?

✔ **How is** .... like planning a summer holiday?

✔ **How is**.......... like repairing a puncture on a tyre?

✔ **How is**.......... like putting up a tent?

✔ **How is**.......... like ringing a call centre?

Fill in your motivational challenge in the space provided and find the associations between your challenge and the simile.

Choose one of the above similes and individually or in small groups come up with as many associations as you can.

After playing this game you're likely to be surprised at the number of creative ideas you've discovered for boosting your motivation. Not only will you come up with some creative ideas, but you'll also have a laugh at the associations. This exercise can also help you to understand how sometimes, like ringing a call centre, you feel as if you're wasting lots of time and going around in circles. You may find yourself coming up with different and more productive approaches for your personal challenge.

Take the example of the challenge of studying for your exams. Instead of putting off getting started by finding lots of excuses, have fun and link your challenge with planning a summer holiday. The summer holiday is like the reward after completing your exams. Prior to going on holiday you need to decide where you are going (which exams), when to travel (dates of the exams), and prepare what you'll need (your revision plan). Your holiday packing is similar to the preparation for your exams. So take a moment now and prepare a revision plan and make a commitment to start some revision today, just as if you were taking action to plan and book your holiday.

After the success of your exams, you can then celebrate and go on holiday after all!

Thinking Like a Child

Young children love asking questions and always want answers. They have an insatiable curiosity. As you grow up, you start imposing rules and regulations, and forgetting how to let your hair down, staying curious, or wanting to try out new things.

To help you look at things from a child's perspective, ask yourself this question: 'How would a 6-year-old boy set about motivating himself?'

Pretend you are 6 years old. What is going on around you? Do you notice things that you didn't see as an adult? Looking at the world with a child's eyes can help you see alternative pathways to reaching your goals, as well as taking down some of the rigid barriers that adults often impose on themselves and on others.

Taking the Brain's Perspective

Ned Herrmann's work on *thinking styles* highlights different thinking preferences that you can use to tackle certain tasks. Thinking styles show how you think, learn, communicate, and make decisions based on different thinking preferences.

Table 17-1 lists the four preferences. Each preference is given a colour; two focusing on skills from the left side of the brain and two focusing on skills from the right side of the brain.

Table 17-1	Thinking Styles
Left-side of brain thinking preference or dominance	*Right-side of brain thinking preference or dominance*
BLUE Using analytical data	YELLOW
Gathering facts and figures	Having vision
Being a technology buff	Coming up with ideas
Exploring financial data	Taking risks
	Playing games
GREEN	RED
Being organised	Focusing on people
Following procedures	Being supportive
Planning	Willing to communicate
Using systems	Feeling for others
Monitoring results	

Adapted from the HBDI (Herrmann Brain Dominance Instrument) and The Whole Brain Business Book by Ned Herrmann, McGraw Hill ©1996. The red/blue/green/yellow colour scheme is a trademark, owner Herrmann International, and is used here with permission.

Take the thinking styles analysis in Table 17-1 and think about how you can use it to help you maintain your motivation. You can also carry out a personal profile via the Herrmann International website (see Appendix).

You can have lots of fun imagining how you'd tackle certain tasks based on Table 17-1. Take the example of tackling a new project:

- ✔ **Blue thinking preference.** You'd be interested in collecting all the facts and figures about the project, the costs involved, and information about any technological issues which may arise.

- ✔ **Green thinking preference.** You'd be very organised in your approach to the project, putting time aside, planning the milestones, and following any set procedures.

✔ **Red thinking preference.** You'd communicate clearly with everyone so they knew what was happening. You'd make sure everyone received up-to-date information, speaking to people, and ensuring that everyone was part of the project.

✔ **Yellow thinking preference.** You'd come up with ideas, have fun, and think of creative approaches to the project. You may come up with wacky and inventive ideas.

Decide which colour you found easier to consider and play with. Often people have a preference for two or three colours or even an element of each. Knowing which colour felt the hardest to deal with is also useful, and this is often your least favourite area. Sometimes you do need to consider your least favourite preference, and either get someone to help you or decide to dip your toe in the water to have a go.

Drawing a Motivated Person

This is a fun and fast exercise – you have to literally be quick on the draw. This exercise encourages you to think visually about motivation and helps you see the way your behaviour can impact another person's motivation.

This exercise can be done individually or with four to five people. You need a flip chart and coloured and scented pens!

Give yourself five minutes to draw a picture of a well-motivated person or a very poorly motivated person. Think of someone you know who shows some of the characteristics you're depicting. Include as many of the senses as possible in the picture; for example, what the person in the drawing is seeing, hearing, and feeling to help show if the person is motivated or demotivated.

When the five minutes are up, and if you're working in groups, have each group present its ideas to the whole room. Hold up your drawing and point out what you've discovered about the motivation of the person you've drawn. Does your drawing highlight characteristics that you haven't been aware of up to now?

If you're working on your own, take a moment to admire your art work and consider whether other people see you as a motivated person or not when you meet up with them. What characteristics would you like to show more or less of?

A variation of this exercise uses the theme of 'dressing up' or 'acting out'. This is fun to do with a friend and whatever clothes or props you can find around the house. Decide if you're going to act or dress up as a motivated or very demotivated person. Have fun as you explore the different characteristics. Again, take a moment to consider how you could portray more motivation in how you look, what you say, what people observe in you. Chat through the ideas with your friend.

Using Role Models

You can do this exercise on your own, in pairs, or in small groups. It's a game of reflection. Ask yourself the following questions:

- If you think of a highly motivated person, who springs to mind?
- What characteristics about that person resonate with you?
- Which of the person's traits or styles do you wish you could have?
- How motivated do you feel when you think about the person?
- How does the person make you feel?
- What aspects of the person's life would you like to copy?
- What can you discover from the person?
- What are you going to try for yourself first?

Taking a Different Approach

> *No problem can be solved from the same consciousness that created it. We must learn to see the world anew.*
>
> —Albert Einstein

Taking a different approach helps you change your perspective on situations, providing new ideas and often new solutions. It prevents you becoming too set in your ways and resistant to change. A new approach can also help to increase your motivation by seeing a situation in a new light.

The following individual exercise is adapted from Positiveworks Ltd (see Appendix). The aim is to encourage you to do something different every day to help inspire motivation as you look at the world afresh from a new perspective.

The following list gives you some ideas for stretching your imagination, leaving your comfort zone, and trying out something new.

✔ Change your morning routine.

✔ Wear a different outfit.

✔ Eat different food for breakfast.

✔ Take a different route to work.

✔ Treat your colleagues differently.

✔ Change your office or home layout.

✔ Bring colour into your thinking at work.

✔ Buy something unusual to eat or go to a different place for lunch.

✔ Talk to a member of staff you have rarely spoken to before.

✔ Think of something your colleagues do not know about you and share it.

✔ Look at your products or services and think up some zany new ideas.

✔ Get home on time to play a silly game with your children.

✔ Be a little more frivolous than usual.

✔ Treat your partner to something romantic and different.

✔ Watch the sunset.

✔ Bathe, shower, or wash with your eyes closed.

✔ Clean your teeth or shave with your other hand . . . with care!

✔ Watch TV with the sound off.

Which of the things from the list did you choose to do? Has doing different things helped free your mind and given you a different approach to getting yourself motivated?

Creating a Motivational Resource Bank

This exercise encourages you to think what resources you need around you to feel motivated. Draw a diagram like the one in Figure 17-1 by adding words or pictures to show the resources you think you need based on a particular goal you have.

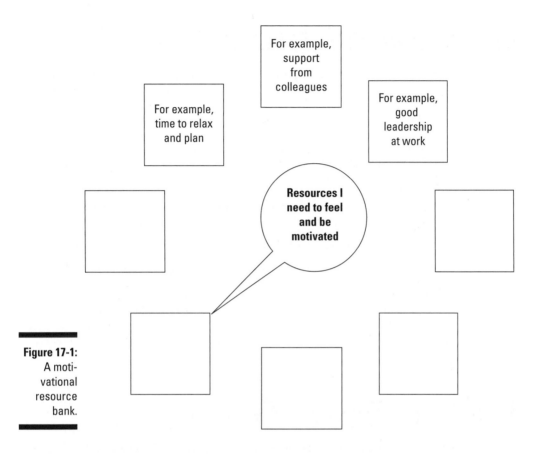

Figure 17-1:
A moti-
vational
resource
bank.

For example, you may feel that the following resources are important to you depending on your personal goal.

- ✔ A relaxing environment
- ✔ Supportive friends
- ✔ Time for exercise and relaxation
- ✔ Maintaining a balance between your home and work life
- ✔ The opportunity to develop new skills or enhance existing ones

Now add your own to the diagram based on your personal goal.

Having Fun with Pictures

This exercise is particularly good for large teams of people. It comes from Linda Denny, a Personal and Business Coach who runs the Smart Coaching Company (see Appendix). Many organisations, including a major airline, have used the exercise with great success for team building and motivation.

You need a selection of magazines, journals, catalogues, and newspapers. You also need a large sheet of flip-chart paper and scissors and glue for each group. Then, follow these steps:

1. **Each group of three to five people is given the task of creating a collage to show what motivates them in all areas of their life.**

   Each group is given 20 to 30 minutes to make the collage.

2. **Each group then presents their collage to the whole room and the key points from the collages are then collated.**

The benefit of the exercise is that team members have the opportunity of talking about what personally motivates them and having the chance of discovering motivating factors that they hadn't come across or considered before.

Motivation Through Exercise

The following group exercise is used by Greg Searle. Greg won an Olympic Gold Medal at the 1992 Olympic Games in Barcelona alongside his brother Jonny in the men's rowing pairs. He also won a Bronze Medal in the Coxless Four at the 1996 Atlanta Olympic Games, and was an Olympic finalist in the Coxless Pair in Sydney 2000.

Following his retirement from international rowing, Greg joined the British America's Cup team as a Grinder in the 2002 Challenger Series. Greg now works as a performance consultant and portfolio director for Lane4 Management Group, an international performance development consultancy. Greg draws upon his experience of elite performance sport to specialise in the fields of performance leadership, team development and motivation, performance coaching, and psychological preparation for performance. Lane4 specialises in programmes providing learning and performance development for organisations worldwide (see Appendix).

1. **Create a space at the front of the room – the left is for those people who hate exercise, the right is for those people who love exercise.**

   You can also add a middle **unsure zone** for those people who feel they are somewhere in the middle!

2. **Ask each participant to stand in whichever space applies to them in relation to loving or hating exercise, or not knowing.**

3. **Ask each participant the following questions:**

   - Why are they standing in that section?

   - What do they love or hate about exercise?

   - What makes them think they love or hate exercise?

   - What level of determination are they showing?

   - What makes them stick at their task?

   - What goals do they have?

   - What choices do they have?

   - Which people are like them?

4. **Ask each participant what would have to happen to make them move toward the opposite group: *hate* to *love* exercise, *love* to *hate* exercise or to move from the middle zone.**

5. **Ask the participants to look for similarities in how they tackle or describe their thoughts on exercise to their tasks in their daily job.**

   Are there any similarities? Are there some things they love about exercise (for example, meeting with mates after work for a game of football, or in Greg's case having a row on the river!). Examples of similarities can be:

   - Enjoying team sports or exercise and wanting to feel more part of the team at work.

   - Loving the competitive aspect of exercise and wanting to be more competitive at work.

   - Hating being competitive and doing exercise, and just wanting a 9 to 5 job that earns them the money to pay their bills.

After capturing the key points from the exercise, note the points on a flip chart, as shown in Table 17-2.

Table 17-2	Loving or Hating Exercise	
Hate exercise	*Middle zone*	*Love exercise*
Step 3: Capture key reasons	Step 3: Capture key reasons	Step 3: Capture key reasons
Step 4: What would have to happen to make you move to the other groups?	Step 4: What would have to happen to make you move to either group?	Step 4: What would have to happen to make you move to the other groups?
Step 5: Highlight similarities with work	Step 5: Highlight similarities with work	Step 5: Highlight similarities with work

Loving or hating exercise is useful for this activity as most people can relate to the subject. The activity helps you understand clearly what you love or hate about exercise and how what you have highlighted can be linked to making changes in your job to increase your motivation.

As a variation, you could do this exercise on your own considering where you would stand and how you would answer the questions. You could also get a group of friends together one evening at home and work through the exercise considering the aspects that link into your personal motivation.

Playing the Game of Reversal

You can play the motivational game of reversal on your own, with small groups of five or six people, or with larger groups of up to 12 people at a time, although working with other people in this exercise often stimulates more ideas than doing it on your own. This game is adapted from a creativity exercise used by Illumine Training Ltd (see Appendix).

First of all you need to ask the following question: What do I have to do to be completely lacking in motivation?

1. **In groups of five to six or in a group of 12 ask everyone to come up with as many ideas that they can think of to answer the reversed question.**

   Allow about 5 minutes for Step 1 of the exercise.

2. **Ask one of the group to write down what each person says, making sure that every comment is noted (however daft it may sound!).**

3. **Now answer the reverse question: What do I have to do to be as motivated as possible?**

4. **Staying in the same groups ask everyone to come up with as many ideas that they can think of to answer the new question.**

   It is important to encourage each person to be creative, rather than just thinking of directly opposite answers to Step 1.

5. **Again allow about 5 minutes for Step 3 of the exercise.**

   This time ask another person in the group to do the writing and make sure that every comment is carefully noted as before. Don't question any of the comments.

6. **Each person in the group now looks at the comments from Step 3.**

   Give each person in the group a different coloured pen, and ask each person to highlight in the list the three most important things they can do to keep themselves as motivated as possible.

   At the end of Step 3 see which of the ideas has been highlighted the most. You may find a clear winner or two or three great ideas which can then be put into action to help motivate the team.

The benefit of the exercise is that it encourages team members to come up with creative ideas for motivation by initially thinking of the negative side first.

The game of reversal is a powerful technique and also designed to make everyone laugh! Now create your own chart of comments relating to the reversal question, as shown in the example in Table 17-3.

Table 17-3	Playing the Game of Reversal
What do I have to do to be completely lacking in motivation?	**What do I have to do to be as motivated as possible?**
Mark all the comments from Step 1 here, for example:	Mark all the comments from Step 2 here, for example:
Feeling miserable	Go for it
Not willing to participate	Being prepared to make mistakes
Believing it's not possible	Taking a risk
Don't share any ideas	Knowing it's okay to fail
Feel like a failure	Talking to positive people
Not willing to have a go	Breaking the goal into manageable chunks

Six Words Motivational Exercise

Yes, I realise this is exercise number 11, but I felt it was a much too powerful exercise to leave out! It may be the shortest exercise, but it can have a lot of impact.

In the 1920s, Ernest Hemingway bet ten dollars that he could write a complete story in just six words. He wrote: 'For Sale: baby shoes, never worn.' He won the bet.

This exercise is based on a BBC Radio interview 'Life in Six Words', where the person being interviewed is asked to sum up their life in just *six* words.

You need to whittle down what you want to say into six words: what you do, what values you have, what inspires and motivates you. The exercise helps you to think very specifically about what is really important to you and what really motivates you.

For example, 'Inspiring healthy minds and healthy bodies'.

Chapter 18

Ten Daily Actions for Keeping Your Motivation High

*T*aking a few moments each and every day to feed your motivation can help you to maintain your enthusiasm and commitment and keep you working positively towards your goals. In this chapter, I suggest some great daily actions you can take to keep you on track and to remind you how to keep your motivation well and truly high!

As you follow each daily tip, enjoy the feeling of extra motivation and the satisfaction of knowing that you're making progress towards your goal, however big or small.

Keeping Focused On Your End Goal

Having a clear end goal in mind and continually reinforcing that goal by staying focused on it can help you make those important changes in your life and maintain your motivation to keep going, even when reaching your goal seems a long way off. Consider the following questions every day to make sure your end goal stays very clear in your mind:

- ✔ What do you really want?
- ✔ How will achieving your goal affect you?
- ✔ Will achieving your goal make a big change to your life?
- ✔ What will the benefits be for you and others around you?
- ✔ How important is achieving your goal to you?
- ✔ Are you capable of achieving what you want?
- ✔ Do you have the time and inclination to dedicate to working towards your goal?
- ✔ Is a cost involved and is it affordable?

Remember to write down your goal. Doing this helps you to clarify specifically what your goal actually is, and helps you to detail the key elements involved in achieving your goal. If you're struggling to put pen to paper, bear in mind that this process can highlight aspects of your goal that may need further definition and clarity.

Taking Time Out to Speak with Your Friends

When you've decided your goal (and written it down!), taking time to speak to your friends about it can act as a great morale booster. The process of verbalising the goal to others helps to clarify different stages and elements that you've not sufficiently thought through, or even not thought of at all, and can help you to focus clearly on your goal. Speaking about your intention with friends also helps you to assess whether it's achievable and if you have sufficient commitment to leave the starting block and take action.

Conversations with friends not only give you the opportunity to define key details and milestones, but you may also find that you need to change the focus of your goal in some way to highlight a new approach you'd not previously considered.

After speaking to your friends, you may need to review your goal again and make some changes. Doing this is fine, and is part of the refining process that helps to maintain your motivation in the long term.

When I run motivational courses, I initially ask people to write down their key goals, usually in the form of a picture. When they pair up with another delegate to talk about the issue they often think of different ideas and information to add to their project or goal, bringing it alive and making it more realistic for them. When the other delegate knows what they are working on, they too can offer daily encouragement to help them move forward.

Planning Your Time

Planning and setting aside time each day to do something towards your goal can help to maintain your motivation as you see things progressing, however slowly. Setting *realistic* deadlines and targets to work towards helps you to feel that you're gradually getting closer to your goal, bit by bit. This helps to keep your motivation high to keep going. The way you do this can be as simple as saying 'by Friday I want to have done this element of my goal', or 'by my next birthday my goal is to…'. Building this time frame element into your day helps you to realise that you are making progress and that you can achieve the targets you've set for yourself.

Plans can be in your mind, but writing them down with key milestones and time scales makes them much more effective. Sticking to your plan by stopping distractions taking over is obviously important, giving you a clear pathway to follow so that you finish the project.

Write the key milestones in your diary, in a list, or on a project plan, and put them in a prominent place so you can refer to it easily and regularly. For example, stick your plan on the fridge door or on your desk top so you can see and review it every day.

Having Contingency Plans in Place

Planning for the unexpected by working out some contingency plans to have in place helps you to keep moving forward, providing you with alternative options if something doesn't go quite according to plan. Think of it like taking an umbrella or a rain coat to an outdoor function. You hope you'll never need the umbrella, but if you don't have it with you, you can guarantee that you'll get rained on!

Contingency plans can include finding extra resources, asking other people to help, and devising different time frames. What is appropriate as a contingency plan at the start of your journey may not work so well as you get closer to achieving your goal, so be creative, be realistic, and regularly spend time thinking about alternative ways of achieving what you want.

To work out a contingency plan, think about what could go wrong and come up with some alternative options or different time scales to consider. Then, you'll still be able to move forward, even when some unexpected obstacles get in the way of achieving what you want.

When I write an article for work, or even a chapter for this book, to help maintain my motivation I use the contingency plan of putting aside more time than I realistically require. In addition, I schedule time in over several days to allow for thinking and creative time, rather than expecting my creative juices to flow constantly!

Tuning Into Your Intuition

Listening to your intuition is about tuning into your feelings to see if you need to consider other aspects of your goal or task. You can tune into your intuition by sleeping on an issue or even going for a walk as you consider an aspect which may be causing you some challenge.

Tuning into your intuition enables your unconscious mind to start working on the problem for you when you're not consciously thinking about it yourself. You need to listen to your inner voice to see what other messages your mind and body may have for you to help keep your motivation high. Be prepared to make some changes if necessary.

Tuning into your intuition can also mean paying attention to your gut reaction and sensing how something feels. For example, if you sense that something doesn't feel quite right, you need to respond to that feeling and take appropriate action.

Knowing the Value of Half Time

Allowing yourself some time out to take stock of how you're getting on and to review your progress towards your goal helps to maintain your motivation. You can check how you're getting on and make adjustments as required, to keep working positively towards your goal. For example, think of the manager of a football team deciding in half time on a different approach for the second half, or a tennis player taking time between sets to recharge, allowing them a brief rest to regain energy and a chance to give their body food and fuel ready for the second half.

Half time with motivation and goals works in a similar way and provides the opportunity to change tack if any key elements aren't working or if you feel you're getting stuck in a rut and not moving anywhere. For example, imagine being stuck in a traffic jam where you feel you're getting nowhere. After a 'half-time think', your motivation to get to your destination remains strong and you decide to leave the motorway at the next junction, take a break, or even travel by a different route. Doing this may take longer, but often ensures that you keep moving – a better feeling than just being stuck in a queue getting frustrated.

Symbolically, half time is allowing your body and mind to have a rest. Consider taking a walk, having some exercise, and reviewing where you are and where you still need to get to.

Dealing with Your Fears

Some people have specific fears about achieving their particular goals. Take the example of someone whose goal is to improve their swimming, yet he is petrified of having his head under water. Facing his fear by swimming with goggles initially may be all that he needs to do, so he gets used to water around his face.

To ensure that you're able to keep proceeding towards your goals, confronting any fears that you have head on and addressing them when they first occur to you is important. If you don't, the fear will constantly niggle away at you and could derail your progress towards your goal.

Consider whether anything is stopping you or slowing you down, or if aspects of your plan concern you. Voicing a fear, problem, or worry and trying to answer your questions can help clarify a key element which otherwise may be preventing you from achieving your goal.

Dealing with your fears may necessitate you doing something quite different and being prepared to take a risk if necessary, even if your initial approach doesn't work. Failure and bouncing back are key elements for keeping some people motivated, and failure is a learning tool in itself!

Leaving a fear unresolved hinders progress towards achieving your ultimate goal.

Doing Something Enjoyable Towards Your Goal

Committing to a daily action keeps your task and goal uppermost in your mind, and ensures that you feed your project regularly, just as you eat regular meals every day to maintain your energy and well-being. Not only is doing something towards your goal every day important for actually achieving it, but making sure that what you do is enjoyable helps to maintain your motivation to get there. Having fun and feeling happy in what you do, ensuring that you have a laugh and bringing in some fun elements, always helps to keep people in a positive frame of mind.

Doing something, however small, each day helps you to slowly eat away at your key tasks or your goal. For example, just making a phone call for some information, making contact with someone you need to speak to, or fulfilling a task that you need to do so you can move onto the next stage are all small steps, but each one is a step closer towards your goal.

All goals, however big or small, are really just a series of bite-sized chunks. Tackling them one step at a time helps to maintain your motivation.

Keeping Your Confidence High

Keeping your confidence high and giving your self esteem a boost can help to keep you on track. Taking time each day to review your successes to date can give you that boost and encourage you to keep progressing forward, especially during times when your energy feels low.

Consider whether anything else can boost your confidence to tackle the goal or your task at hand, such as speaking through your progress to date with a colleague who you can rely on to be full of praise and encouragement. Refer back to the questions you answered in the 'Keeping Focused On Your End Goal' section earlier in this chapter about making sure your goal is clear and remind yourself that you've already decided that this goal is perfectly achievable. Remind yourself on a daily basis that you can do it!

Rewarding Yourself for Successes along the Way

Regularly building in rewards as you work towards your goal, as well as at the end, helps keep your enjoyment about achieving your goal or task uppermost in your mind. Rewards are particularly important for encouraging you to keep going if you start to feel low at any time. Choose rewards that are personally motivating for you; they are different for each person.

You can link rewards to key milestones. For example, if your goal is to lose 2 stone in weight, ask a friend to take a photo of you after each 7-pound loss. Stick the photo on your fridge so you can see and take pride in your progress each day, and treat yourself to a reward. You could also leave out on show an outfit that's now obviously too big for you as a great motivator to remind you how well you're doing.

Appendix

Resource List

● ●

*I*n this appendix you find a selection of books, and training and coaching websites that can help you on your motivation journey. There simply isn't room here to list every book, article, or organisation involved in motivation. If you're keen to find out even more, your best move is to search the Internet.

If you want to get in touch, you can find me at Health Circles Ltd, Tel: +44 (0) 1628 666 069; email `gillianburn@healthcircles.co.uk`; and `www. healthcircles.co.uk`.

Books

When you've finished reading through *Motivation For Dummies* (and of course, reading through it a second time, to get your full value), the following books can help you hone your motivation skills even further.

Building Self-Confidence For Dummies by Kate Burton and Brinley N. Platts (Wiley)

Effective Motivation: How to Get Extraordinary Results from Everyone (Effective Series) by John Adair (Macmillan)

Maximum Achievement: Strategies and Skills That Will Unlock Your Hidden Powers to Succeed by Brian Tracy (Simon & Schuster)

Mindset: The New Psychology of Success by Carol S. Dweck (Random House)

Neuro-linguistic Programming For Dummies by Romilla Ready and Kate Burton (Wiley)

Performance Coaching For Dummies by Gladeana McMahon and Averil Leimon (Wiley)

Reinventing Yourself: How to Become the Person You've Always Wanted to Be by Steve Chandler (Career Press)

Self-theories: Their Role in Motivation, Personality, and Development by Carol S. Dweck (Essays in Social Psychology) (Psychology Press)

The Big Book of Motivation Games by Robert Epstein and Jessica Rogers (McGraw-Hill)

The Inner Game of Work: Overcoming Mental Obstacles for Maximum Performance by Timothy Gallwey (Texere Publishing)

Motivation Pocketbook by Max A. Eggert (Management Pocketbooks)

100 Ways to Motivate Yourself: Change Your Life Forever by Steve Chandler (Career Press)

What's My Motivation by D. Griffin (BookSurge Publishing)

Training and Coaching Websites

The following organisations specialise in training and coaching. You can contact them via their website addresses. I list the organisations alphabetically:

Businessballs: www.businessballs.com. This website provides motivational materials including ice-breakers, team-building games, quotations, and motivational activities. It also contains information on motivation and learning theories.

Fenman Ltd: www.fenman.co.uk/cat/product_info/mmw4.pdf; Tel: +44 (0)1353 665533, Fax: +44 (0) 1353 663644. Fenman's website provides motivational resources and practical exercises including step-by-step trainer's notes for running motivational exercises. Resources include training DVDs, videos, manuals, and games for learning and development professionals to use that you can purchase directly via the www.fenman.co.uk website.

Fresh Tracks: www.freshtracks.co.uk; Tel: +44 (0) 1920 822 220. Fresh Tracks programmes focus on three key principles for success including fun, attitudes, and relationships. The company offers conferences, team-building programmes, and in-house consultations to business teams for groups of from 12 to 1,200. You can find additional team exercises, ice-breakers, and energisers at www.trainerstoolkit.co.uk.

Health Circles Ltd: www.healthcircles.co.uk; Tel: +44 (0) 1628 666 069, Fax: +44 (0) 1628 666 069. My website, offering programmes to improve health and quality of life by creating healthy minds and bodies.

Herrmann International: www.HerrmannInternational.com; Tel: +1 828 625 9153, Fax: +1 828 625 1402. Creator and exclusive provider of the HBDI (Herrmann Brain Dominance Instrument). Provides information on validated thinking styles analysis: what it is, how it can be used, completing a personal profile, and information on training courses.

Illumine Ltd: www.illumine.co.uk; Tel: +44 (0) 1753 866 633, Fax: +44 (0) 1753 866 640. A premier UK training organisation, providing training to enhance practical thinking skills to improve the performance of individuals and organisations. The range of courses covers: assimilation, innovation, communication, facilitation, and motivation.

Lane4 Management Group Ltd (Europe): www.lane4.co.uk; Tel: +44 (0) 1628 533733, Fax: +44 (0) 1628 533766. A leading international performance development consultancy offering a wide range of activities, focusing on creating transformational learning, leading to enhanced performance at organisational, team, and individual levels. Programmes include: interactive experiential workshops, focused team-development events, organisational performance measurement, and senior executive coaching.

Management For The Rest of Us: www.mftrou.com/group-team-building-activity.html. Management articles and resources for team building and personal development including games, ice-breakers, activities, and information on challenge days and business games.

Positiveworks Ltd: www.positiveworks.com; Tel: +44 (0) 207 736 1417, Fax: +44 (0) 207 731 5399. Focuses on developing people. Positiveworks aims to change your development initiatives by providing coaching, development programmes, and facilitation services specifically tailored to the business and personal objectives of clients.

Smart Coaching Company: www.thesmartcoachingcompany.com; Tel: +44 (0) 1753 645754. Specialises in leadership, productivity and career coaching, mentoring for groups, and one to one. Smart Coaching's approach is simple and practical, with a style that is passionate, entrepreneurial, supportive, and solution focused.

Stanford University, Department of Psychology: www-psych.stanford.edu; Tel: +1 650 725 2400, Fax: +1 650 725 5699. This website offers research articles covering intelligence, motivation, and learning including the motivation of achievement, left brain/right brain research, the effect of mindsets, and self-esteem.

The Centre for Stress Management: www.managingstress.com; Tel: +44 (0) 20 8228 1185, Fax: +44 (0) 20 8228 1186. An international training centre and stress consultancy. Carries out stress management and prevention programmes, stress audits and research, stress counselling, coaching, and training.

Index

• *S* •

Notes

Notes

Notes

Notes

Notes

Notes

Notes

Notes

FOR DUMMIES®

Do Anything. Just Add Dummies

UK editions

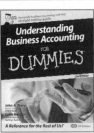

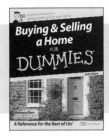
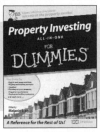

FOR DUMMIES®

A world of resources to help you grow

UK editions

SELF-HELP

Cognitive Behavioural Therapy For Dummies
978-0-470-01838-5

Neuro-linguistic Programming For Dummies
978-0-7645-7028-5

Personal Development All-in-One For Dummies
978-0-470-51501-3

HEALTH

Stop Smoking For Dummies
978-0-470-99456-6

IBS For Dummies
978-0-470-51737-6

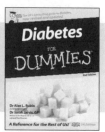
Diabetes For Dummies
978-0-470-05810-7

HISTORY

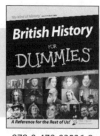
British History For Dummies
978-0-470-03536-8

Twentieth Century History For Dummies
978-0-470-51015-5

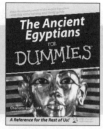
The Ancient Egyptians For Dummies
978-0-470-06544-0

Hypnotherapy For Dummies
978-0-470-01930-6

Inventing For Dummies
978-0-470-51996-7

Job Hunting and Career Change All-in-One For Dummies
978-0-470-51611-9

Motivation For Dummies
978-0-470-76035-2

Origami Kit For Dummies
978-0-470-75857-1

Patents, Registered Designs, Trade Marks and Copyright For Dummies
978-0-470-51997-4

Psychometric Tests For Dummies
978-0-470-75366-8

Raising Happy Children For Dummies
978-0-470-05978-4

Starting and Running a Business All-in-One For Dummies
978-0-470-51648-5

Sudoku For Dummies
978-0-470-01892-7

The British Citizenship Test For Dummies, 2nd Edition
978-0-470-72339-5

Time Management For Dummies
978-0-470-77765-7

Wills, Probate, & Inheritance Tax For Dummies, 2nd Edition
978-0-470-75629-4

Winning on Betfair For Dummies, 2nd Edition
978-0-470-72336-4

12816_p2

Available wherever books are sold. For more information or to order direct go to www.wiley.com or call +44 (0) 1243 843291

FOR DUMMIES®

The easy way to get more done and have more fun

LANGUAGES

978-0-7645-5194-9

Speak French — the fun and easy way!

French FOR DUMMIES

978-0-7645-5193-2

Start speaking Italian

Italian FOR DUMMIES

978-0-7645-5196-3

MUSIC

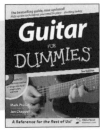

978-0-7645-9904-0

DJing FOR DUMMIES

978-0-470-03275-6
UK Edition

Piano FOR DUMMIES

978-0-7645-5105-5

SCIENCE & MATHS

978-0-7645-5326-4

Chemistry FOR DUMMIES

978-0-7645-5430-8

Algebra FOR DUMMIES

978-0-7645-5325-7

Art For Dummies
978-0-7645-5104-8

Baby & Toddler Sleep Solutions For Dummies
978-0-470-11794-1

Bass Guitar For Dummies
978-0-7645-2487-5

Christianity For Dummies
978-0-7645-4482-8

Filmmaking For Dummies
978-0-7645-2476-9

Forensics For Dummies
978-0-7645-5580-0

German For Dummies
978-0-7645-5195-6

Hobby Farming For Dummies
978-0-470-28172-7

Jewelry Making & Beading For Dummies
978-0-7645-2571-1

Judaism For Dummies
978-0-7645-5299-1

Knitting For Dummies, 2nd Edition
978-0-470-28747-7

Music Composition For Dummies
978-0-470-22421-2

Physics For Dummies
978-0-7645-5433-9

Sex For Dummies, 3rd Edition
978-0-470-04523-7

Solar Power Your Home For Dummies
978-0-470-17569-9

Tennis For Dummies
978-0-7645-5087-4

The Koran For Dummies
978-0-7645-5581-7

U.S. History For Dummies
978-0-7645-5249-6

Wine For Dummies, 4th Edition
978-0-470-04579-4

12816_p3

FOR DUMMIES®

Making Everything Easier

Our Bestselling Titles

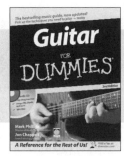
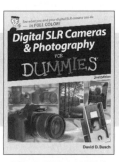

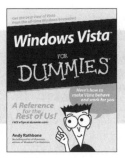

FOR DUMMIES®

Making Everything Easier

Our Bestselling Titles

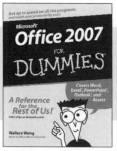

978-0-470-00923-9

978-0-471-77774-8

978-0-7645-3758-5

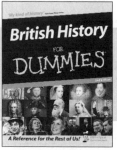

978-0-470-03536-8

978-0-470-12174-0

978-0-470-14928-7

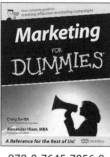

978-0-7645-7056-8

978-0-470-24055-7

978-0-470-51648-5

978-0-7645-5434-6

978-0-470-03135-3

978-0-7645-5193-2

13941_p2